Western Europe
after Hitler

Titles in this series

MODERN TIMES

Western Europe after Hitler

B. J. Elliott

LONGMAN

LONGMAN GROUP LIMITED
London
Associated companies, branches and representatives throughout the world

© Longman Group Ltd (formerly Longmans, Green & Co Ltd) 1968

First published 1968
Sixth impression 1977

ISBN 0 582 20436 4

Printed in Hong Kong by
Sheck Wah Tong Printing Press

Acknowledgements

For permission to reproduce photographs we are grateful to the following:

Associated Newspapers Ltd pp. xi, 89; Keystone Press Agency pp. xii, 3, 7, 11, 12, 13, 16, 20, 26, 28, 35, 37, 41, 44, 46, 50, 52, 54, 57, 63, 67, 70, 72, 78, 80, 81, 85, 88, 93, 99, 101, 103, 111, 113, 118, 120, 122, 126, 127, 133 and 138; Aufnahme der Landesbildstelle Berlin pp. 31 and 97; European Community Information Service pp. 60, 61, 136 and 142; Sovfoto p. 74; *The Guardian* p. 104; Crown copyright p. 115; Bippa pp. 129 and 151; Hawker Siddeley p. 146 and Cassell & Co. Ltd for a map from *Berlin Airlift* by Robert Rodrigo.

Contents

Preface

During the last quarter-century Europe has undergone a series of far-reaching political and economic changes. The continent which once dominated the world, became in 1945 the arena in which the two super-powers face each other with distrust and suspicion.

Europeans in the West, deprived of their enormous Afro-Asian Empires, have turned inwards to seek a unity unknown since the Roman Empire. In the East, the monolithic Empire of Stalin has crumbled and Europeans have developed a new individualism and closer links with the West.

These are the themes I have tried to expand but since they form a story which is still evolving it is neither possible to draw firm conclusions nor wise to make predictions. For the future one must hope that Europeans can rise above the selfish nationalism which so often has been the 'gravedigger' of the Continent. This will be achieved only if Europe can avoid becoming a battleground for the third time in this century.

I am indebted to Dr Leslie James M.A. of the Board of Extra-Mural Studies at the University of Cambridge for his penetrating and constructive criticisms and to Mrs M. Garforth for her speedy and accurate production of the typescript.

B. J. ELLIOTT

Time Chart

	NATIONAL DEVELOPMENTS	UNITY MOVEMENTS	COLD WAR	SOVIET BLOC	AFRO-ASIA
1945	Lab. Govt. in U.K.		Potsdam Conference		Indonesian Revolt
46	Italy Republic				War in Indo-China
47		Dunkirk Treaty	Truman Doctrine		India Independent
48		O.E.E.C.	Berlin Blockade	Czech coup	Burma Independent
49	F.D.R. estab.	N.A.T.O.		D.D.R. estab.	Chinese Revolution
1950		Schuman Plan	Korean War		
51	Cons. Govt. in U.K.				Libya Independent
52			First H-Bomb		
53			Death of Stalin	Berlin Uprising	
54		Collapse of E.D.C.			Dien Bien Phu
1955	F.D.R. and Austria independent	Messina Conf.			
56				Hungarian Revolt	Suez War
57	Macmillan	Treaty of Rome		Sputnik 1	Ghana Independent
58	Return of De Gaulle				
59		E.F.T.A.	Khrushchev in U.S.A.		
1960			U-2 Crisis		Congo Independent
61		Britain applies to E.E.C.	Berlin Wall	Gagarin in space	
62			Cuban Crisis		Algeria Independent
63	Adenauer's resignation	E.E.C. bars Britain	Test Ban Treaty		
64	Lab. Govt. in U.K.			Fall of Khrushchev	Chinese A-Bomb
1965			U.S. bombs N. Vietnam		Rhodesian U.D.I.
66	Erhard's resignation				
67		De Gaulle again vetoes British application to E.E.C.			3rd Israeli-Arab War
68			Vietnam Peace Talks	Warsaw Pact invasion of Czechoslovakia	

	NATIONAL DEVELOPMENTS	UNITY MOVEMENTS	COLD WAR	SOVIET BLOCK	AFRO-ASIA
1968	Riots and large strikes in France		Vietnam Peace Talks	Invasion of Czechoslovakia	
69	Pompidou and Brandt in office	Hague E.E.C. Summit			
1970	Cons. Govt. in U.K.		Soviet-German Treaty		End of Nigerian Civil War
71	Increasing violence in Ulster				
72	S.P.D. returned to office	British membership of E.E.C. signed.	US-USSR disarmament Treaty Pres. Nixon in China		Chinese entry into UNO
73		Enlargement of E.E.C.	Vietnam Peace Brezhnev in U.S.A.	Death of W. Ulbricht	

Prologue

Surrender at Reims

'The victor will treat them generously'—General Jodl

The thunder of the 'Red Ball Express' convoy died away as
the giant supply lorries headed towards the German frontier.
Only the shrill chorus of nightingales broke the calm of the
warm May night. The white-helmeted military policemen
standing outside the Supreme Commander's headquarters in
the French city of Reims were listening for another sound—
car engines. As the night wore on and the important visitors
became overdue, the M.P.s paced restlessly, to and fro. For in
the early hours of the morning, 7 May 1945, an event of the
greatest importance was to take place. After 2,000 days of
bitter and bloody war the cease-fire and surrender of the
principal enemy was to be signed in this town.

Victory in Europe

Soon after 2 a.m. the first car arrived and delivered two American generals, Walter Bedell Smith, the Allied Chief of Staff, and Carl Spaatz, the U.S.A.A.F. Chief in Europe. They were soon followed by a Russian, Major-General Ivan Susloparov, a Briton, Lieutenant-General Sir Frederick Morgan, and France's Major-General Sevez. The five Allied commanders walked quickly into the College to await the arrival of the German delegation. They did not have long to wait. A long black car pulled up outside the main doors and three uniformed figures stepped out. First was General Alfred Jodl, Hitler's former Chief of Staff. Then came Major Wilhelm Orenius of the Wehrmacht and finally Admiral Hans von Friedeburg.

The three Germans were taken to the Map Room and ushered into reserved chairs around the great conference table. The remaining space in the room was taken up by batteries of cameras, studio lights and cables with crowds of reporters jostling for elbow-room.

After a brief exchange of words large and impressive documents were produced and circulated around the table for signing. At precisely 2.41 a.m. the ceremony was completed. The German Armed Forces had surrendered completely and

General Jodl signs the surrender document

unconditionally to the four victorious Allied powers. The cease-fire was fixed for one minute after midnight the following morning, 8 May.

General Jodl asked for permission to say a few words, and this was granted.

'With this signature', he said, 'the German people and the Armed Forces are for better or for worse delivered into the victors' hand. In this war, which has lasted more than five years, both achieved and suffered more than perhaps any other people in the world. In this hour I can only express the hope that the victor will treat them generously.'

There was no reply.

I The Harvest of War

Damage and Death

'The Awful Ruin of Europe, with all its vanished glories'—W. S. Churchill

From the shores of the Atlantic to the frontiers of Asia, Europe lay ravaged as if by some giant earthquake. Neither age nor sex had protected even the most innocent from death or mutilation in a score of awful forms. The 2,000 days of war had cost the lives of 500 Europeans every hour, most of whom still lie in unmarked graves.

Everywhere was in chaos and disorder. Countless millions had lost their homes and all possessions. A quarter of all the houses in Germany were destroyed or uninhabitable. Great cathedral cities in France, Belgium, Holland and Italy had been reduced almost to rubble. Paris had been saved from Hitler's vengeance by the disobedience of the German commandant, but the ancient capitals of Eastern Europe, Warsaw, Budapest, Belgrade and Leningrad had suffered terrible poundings. Harbour installations and great bridges were smashed beyond repair. Most main roads were either completely blocked by rubble and overturned vehicles, or were open only to single-line traffic. Every main railway line had been a prime target for Allied bombers. The few trains still remaining were filled to capacity and carried passengers on the roof and even clinging to the engines. The great Corinth canal in western Greece had been wrecked by the retreating Germans. They had blocked one entrance by sinking a 3,500-ton ship. They then tipped a large number of railway coaches into it, and finally, they dynamited the banks.

Although the cities had suffered most, agricultural production had been severely affected by the war. Vast areas of farmland had become battlegrounds for the opposing armies.

European wheat production in 1945 was only 30 per cent of the 1938 figures. In France farmers had to wait for clearance by mine-detectors before it was safe to plant crops again. Thousands of acres in Holland were flooded with salt water after the retreating Germans had blown up the sea walls. The *Times* correspondent in Amsterdam reported seeing people collapse with hunger in the streets.

In such conditions, the black market flourished. A second-hand suit sold for £60 in France, an egg cost £1 in Holland and smokers in the Channel Islands had to pay £3 an ounce for tobacco. The standard currency in Germany soon became the cigarette, which would buy twice as much as the wage for a hard day's work clearing rubble.

Across this wilderness marched the legions of the lost. Between 1938 and 1946 some thirty million Europeans were uprooted from their homes. A great many died, but the task of resettling the survivors presented many difficult problems.

Refugees

'I a stranger and afraid'—A. E. Housman

For three weeks the train stood outside Vienna's South Station, and only the dead could be taken off. Soldiers of the Red Army, warmly clad in furs, stamped through the snow beside the line of open cattle trucks to make sure that the living did not escape. For Robert this enforced stay under the grey Austrian sky was but one more episode in a long nightmare.

Robert was eight years old and sick with typhus. For as long as he could remember, he and his family had been on the move. When the Russians had occupied his homeland of Transylvania in 1940 they had trekked westwards through Hungary, Czechoslovakia and Austria. By late 1944 they had found a home in an empty cowshed near Graz. Then once again the Russians had arrived and the family fled to Maribor in Yugoslavia. But Robert and his family were of German descent (*Volksdeutsche*) and received no pity from the Yugoslavs. Parents and children were arrested and separated—many families for ever—and Robert was sent to the infamous children's camp at Ormož. Starvation and disease brought him close to death, but then the war ended and he was packed off on a train to Hungary. By the greatest stroke of fortune, he met his parents again and then moved on—to Vienna.

When the story of the train and the plight of its passengers leaked out, it hit the headlines of the world press. Still the four powers refused permission to the travellers to alight. Meanwhile, they lived on one bowl of food a day and lost most of their clothes when the Russians pillaged the washing line strung along the length of the train.

By Christmas 1945 the Allies had untangled their rules and the train was allowed to move on with its starving, shivering cargo. Robert's story had a happy ending, but only after he had spent four months in hospital and a much longer period in a wretched camp near Salzburg.

For Robert was one of the millions of Europeans uprooted and left homeless by Hitler's war—refugees or displaced persons (D.P.s). There were about eight million D.P.s in Europe

Refugee column from Eastern Europe

when the war ended, mainly slave labourers, but also survivors from the death camps and people like Robert's family who had fled before the Russians. Most returned home voluntarily within a few months, but many thousands refused to go back to their homelands. These were principally the Eastern Europeans—Poles, Yugoslavs, Ukrainians and Russians. Most of these managed to emigrate to North America and Australia, or to find a permanent home in Europe. Denmark resettled 200,000 *Volksdeutsche*. Nevertheless, there remained for many years a hard core of some 300,000 in camps in Germany and Austria who could not be resettled because of age, health or other reasons. They came under the care of the U.N. Commissioner for Refugees.

The Yalta Conference

'*The question is . . . whether Germany has the will to remain in existence*'—Adolf Hitler in December 1944

Less than five weeks after Hitler posed this question, at the moment when his last attack was beginning to fail,[1] a meeting was held at Yalta in southern Russia. Attending this meeting were the leaders of the three victorious powers, Stalin, Churchill and Roosevelt. The main topic for discussion was the future of Germany after its final defeat.

The three leaders had before them two drastic suggestions: that Germany should be divided into three zones of occupation and that her great industries should be permanently dismantled. The scheme to occupy and divide Germany was the work of the European Advisory Council—E.A.C. This was a committee consisting of one leading diplomat from each of the three great powers. They also decided that Berlin, which lay deep within the proposed Russian Zone, should be divided amongst the three powers. Unfortunately the Americans and the British did not ensure that the road, rail and air links between Berlin and their zones would be guaranteed by the Russians. The second scheme to strip Germany of her 'war' industries originated from an American Cabinet committee

[1] The Battle of the Ardennes.

headed by the Secretary of the Treasury, Henry J. Morgen-thau. The plan is generally referred to as the 'Morgenthau Plan'.

Morgenthau, supported by Roosevelt, believed that Germany was responsible for most of the world's troubles, therefore the destruction of her ability to wage war would provide a lasting peace. The Plan recommended that Germany's great factories and steelworks, such as Krupps, should be closed down. The plant and machinery would then be given to Russia and other countries which had suffered under the Nazis.

The Occupation of Germany

The plan for the division of Germany into zones was agreed upon at Yalta. However, when Roosevelt announced that the American troops would be withdrawn from Europe before 1948, Churchill increased his efforts to secure a zone in Germany for France. Churchill knew that Britain was in no condition to undertake the occupation of West Germany and face a possible threat from Russia singlehanded. After some difficulties, it was agreed that the French should take a separate zone, which the Russians insisted should be carved out of the proposed British and American Zones.

Russia was in favour of the Morgenthau Plan. The Russian Foreign Minister, Vyacheslav Molotov, claimed 10,000 million dollars in reparations from Germany. This would take the form of plant and machinery from her factories and payments in goods for ten years. Finally, he requested four million German workers to help in rebuilding Russia's ruined towns. The British were strongly opposed to a scheme which would probably turn Germany into a vast slum. 'What will happen if Germany is reduced to starvation?', Churchill asked, remembering the terrible lesson of the 1920s, when debts and reparations upset the world economy. Roosevelt, now a very sick man and eager to leave Yalta, agreed to Molotov's figure as a 'basis for discussion'.

The 'Big Three' reached a quick agreement on the procedure of the United Nations Organisation, due to hold its first assembly after the defeat of Germany. Roosevelt also agreed to Stalin's long list of conditions in return for Russia's entry into the war against Japan. The major issue which could not be settled at the Yalta Conference was the future of Poland.

The survival of Poland as a free, strong and independent nation had been the immediate cause of World War II. 'Having drawn the sword on behalf of Poland against Hitler's brutal attack, we could never be content with any solution that did not leave Poland a free and independent state', said Churchill, to which Stalin replied: 'Throughout history Poland has been the corridor through which the enemy has passed to Russia. Twice in the last thirty years our enemies—the Germans, have passed through the corridor. Poland should be in a position to shut the door of this corridor by her own force.'

Polish leader Mikolajczyk

After the invasion by Germany, the Polish government fled to London. The Russians refused to recognise the London Poles and in the summer of 1944 they set up a Communist government at Lublin which lay some 100 miles south-east of Warsaw. On 30 July, the leader of the London Poles, Mikolajczyk, arrived in Moscow for talks with Stalin. He was hoping to come to an arrangement by which the London Poles and the Lublin Poles could settle their differences. The main problem was the fixing of Poland's frontiers after war. The Polish Republic had come into existence in 1919 following the collapse of the Empires of Russia, Germany and Austria-Hungary. The eastern frontier of Poland had been fixed along

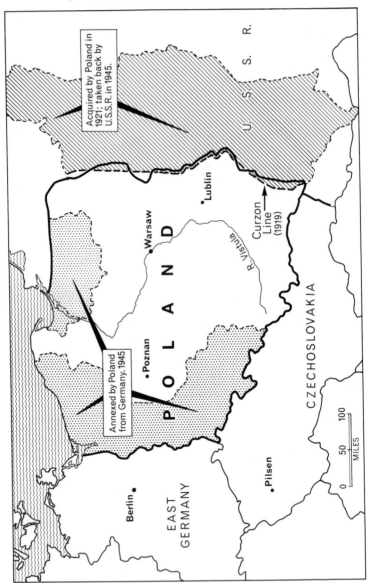

Polish Frontier changes

the so-called Curzon Line (see map above). In 1920 Poland took advantage of Russia's internal troubles to attack her. The war ended with the treaty of Riga, which gave Poland territory from Russia to a depth of about 100 miles. Stalin was determined to recover this territory after the war—although he was willing to compensate Poland with land from Germany. Mikolajczyk knew that the London Poles would never agree to surrender the eastern lands to Russia. For this reason and the fact that Stalin was determined to have a Communist government in Poland, the London and Lublin groups became increasingly hostile. The London Poles also condemned Stalin for his failure to assist the Warsaw uprising in August 1944. A month before the Yalta Conference, Stalin recognised the Lublin group as the temporary government of Poland.

The Western leaders, especially Churchill, pressed Stalin to fix a date for the election of a government. Stalin replied that it would be held 'in about a month'. The Western leaders accepted this promise and agreed that the Polish eastern frontier should return to the 1920 Curzon Line. They also recognised that Poland must be compensated for this with land from Germany; Stalin strongly urged that the Polish–German frontier should run along the rivers Oder and Neisse. Since it was the Red Army which controlled Poland, and would soon overrun East Germany, there could be little doubt that Stalin would have his way.

Three months after the Yalta Conference, Germany was completely defeated and the occupation began.

Germany in the Depths

'*I never saw such destruction*'—President Truman in Berlin, 1945

A FRIGHTFUL DISCOVERY

The police inspector was becoming worried by the number of unexplained disappearances in his small Ruhr town. Even in the turmoil which followed Germany's defeat, the number was unusually high. Then he received a report from one of his men keeping watch at the railway station. An elderly man had been seen there approaching boys and girls and speaking to them for a few moments. Nearly all the young people had then left the station and had not returned. The inspector ordered his man to follow the next boy or girl, and he arranged for several more men to follow at a safe distance. In due course, the elderly man was observed speaking to a girl, obviously a refugee. When he had finished speaking she nodded and walked out of the station. The policeman followed her to a dingy bomb-scarred house in a back street. The girl knocked on the door and was quickly admitted. When, after several minutes, she failed to emerge, the policemen raided the house. In the cellar they found a butcher's shop well stocked with joints of *human* meat! The elderly man had tricked the youngsters into going to the house by telling them that he was waiting for a train but had discovered that he had left his ticket at home. Would they mind fetching it for him?[1]

LANDSCAPE OF DESOLATION

Conditions in Germany at the end of the war were almost beyond description. The inhabitants of great cities like Hamburg were living in cellars, air-raid shelters and holes in the rubble. Only a small number of the original population still clung to their homes—in Frankfurt the figure was 7 per cent. There were no main services; police, fire crews and local government officials had all disappeared. From many trees hung the bodies of 'deserters', 'traitors' and 'defeatists', executed by the S.S. in the last days of the war. When American troops entered Munich they found 10,000 former slave labourers, Polish, French and Russian, running riot through the city. They were plundering the wine shops and warehouses, and wreaking terrible vengeance upon any suspected Nazi who fell into their hands. The Americans who had just liberated Dachau concentration camp were in no mood to save Munich.

More than two-thirds of all the buildings in Berlin had been destroyed or badly damaged by Allied bombs and shells. Vast stretches of the inner city had been completely flattened. Whole streets had disappeared and the inhabitants had taken to the cellars. One great crater, filled with black stinking water, measured 100 yards across. All public transport had halted and the underground railway tunnels were flooded.

Overshadowing all these problems was the shortage of food.

[1] Quoted by Terence Prittie in *Germany Divided* (1960).

War damage, Dresden

Ravaged by war and exhausted by lack of fertilisers and machinery, the farmlands of Germany were totally inadequate for the country's needs. Wolves and wild pigs roamed the countryside sometimes in great packs, smashing fences and uprooting crops. Forbidden to own firearms, the farmers tried to fight them off with bows and arrows. American soldiers went hunting in jeeps using automatic weapons. The occupying forces were responsible for feeding the civilian population but they had neither the will nor the means to do the job satisfactorily. As we have seen, some Germans turned to cannibalism. It was into this landscape of desolation that the leaders of the three great Allied powers arrived in July 1945 at Potsdam, Berlin, to decide finally upon the future of Germany and other important matters.

11

The Potsdam Conference

President Roosevelt had died on 19 April 1945 and was succeeded by the U.S. Vice-President, Harry S. Truman. Churchill arrived at Potsdam on 17 July to represent Britain, but ten days later the result of the General Election was announced. The Labour Party led by Clement Attlee had secured a landslide victory by 180 seats over the Conservative Party. When the Conference resumed on 28 July, therefore, only Stalin of the 'Big Three' wartime leaders survived.

Potsdam Conference—Stalin (1), Truman (2), Attlee (3)

Four major problems occupied the attention of the statesmen who met at Potsdam. The least of these was the entry of Russia into the war against Japan; for on the day before the Conference opened, the Americans successfully exploded the first atomic bomb in New Mexico. There could be little doubt now that Japan would soon be forced to surrender.

The first major European problem was to arrange for the drawing up of peace treaties with the defeated enemy powers —Germany, Italy, Austria, Bulgaria, Finland, Hungary and

Rumania. For this task a Council of Foreign Ministers was set up to meet in London. The Big Three also agreed that France and China should be invited to join the Council although the latter was not to be allowed to vote on European questions.

There was a large measure of agreement about the policy to be adopted in occupied Germany, except over the question of reparations. The British realised that an impoverished Germany would prevent the recovery of Europe, and Truman realised that the Morgenthau Plan would never work. Stalin and Molotov continued to press for 10,000 million dollars,

Stalin and Molotov voting in a Russian election

though they later reduced this figure by 20 per cent. Finally, it was agreed that Russia should be given 15 per cent of all the machinery and plant in the Western Zones in exchange for food and coal from their zone. In addition, they were to receive a further 10 per cent for which they would not have to pay anything.

13

Germany was to be ruled by a Control Council composed of the four Allied Commanders-in-Chief. The purpose of the occupation of Germany was to be:

1. The complete disarmament of Germany and the dismantling of her armament industries.
2. The destruction of the Nazi Party and all its organisations. This included the trials of war criminals.
3. The German people were to be made to realise that they had been utterly defeated.
4. The German people were to be prepared for a return to democratic self-rule and a place in the family of nations.

The major clash, as at Yalta, was over Poland. Stalin's promise of an early general election had not been kept. Instead he had arrested General Okulicki and fourteen other Polish political leaders who had gone to Moscow for talks about the Yalta decisions. All were secretly tried and imprisoned. It was thus quite clear to Churchill and Truman that the areas which the Red Army had overrun were going to remain firmly under Russian control. Ernest Bevin, the new British Foreign Minister, extracted a promise from the leader of the Polish Communists to hold early elections. There was no guarantee that this would be kept, and to this day Poland has a Communist government.

The redrawing of Poland's frontiers was already under way. Millions of Germans had trekked westwards to escape from the advancing Russians and the Polish Government was busy expelling the rest from the areas under dispute. However much Truman, Churchill, and later Attlee, might protest, it was the Red Army that controlled Poland.

The Western leaders therefore made the best terms they could. It was agreed that Germans living in Poland, Czechoslovakia and Hungary should be transferred to Germany in an 'orderly and humane manner'. Until the problems of resettlement had been examined the three governments were asked to suspend transfers of population. Finally it was agreed that the Polish–German frontier should be moved to the Oder-Neisse line as a *temporary* arrangement. In fact, the expulsions were not suspended and some eight million refugees poured into the battered, hungry cities of Germany during 1945 and 1946.

They eventually formed their own political party in West Germany where a Minister for Refugees was appointed. German-drawn maps even today indicate the lost lands in the east as 'under Polish administration' and not as part of Poland.

SUMMARY OF POTSDAM

Potsdam marked the end of America's attempts to come to terms with Russia by making massive concessions. By the end of the Conference, Truman, who had come to act as referee between Churchill and Stalin, was convinced that the latter was 'planning world conquest'. Potsdam also marked the formal end of the 'Grand Alliance', for with Germany defeated, and the surrender of Japan only a week away, there was no longer a reason for the Alliance.

During the long debates between the national leaders many basic and unchangeable differences of opinion had appeared. At that moment the warmth of affection and goodwill created by the Alliance hid this. But as the months and then the years rolled by, the differences between Russia and the West became wider until eventually they broke into unconcealed hostility.

The Remaking of Germany

'*You are sixty-eight and your life is virtually at an end*'—Gestapo Officer to Konrad Adenauer in 1944

High on a hill above the Rhine a lean and leathery-faced old man stood staring across the valley at the opposite bank. He was watching the movements of American troops who were preparing to cross the river and make their final assault upon Germany. Suddenly, he caught sight of a shell hurtling towards him and he flung himself to the ground. The shell landed a dozen yards away and shrapnel whizzed over his prone figure. A second and a third landed even closer but the man was unharmed. Temporarily deafened, he scrambled to his feet and stumbled back to the wine cellar behind his house where fourteen members of his family and three French P.O.W.s were sheltering.

Although the bombardment continued for a week, the house was not hit. It was unsafe to leave the shelter, however, except between 7 and 8 a.m., when the American gunners were having breakfast. Then the firing stopped and on the morning of 15 March 1945 a jeep containing two U.S. Army officers drove up to the house. They addressed the elderly man in perfect German:

'Doctor Konrad Adenauer? We come from General Eisenhower. If you are willing, he wishes to appoint you Oberburgmeister (Lord Mayor) of Cologne!'

OCCUPATION TACTICS

As soon as a town was occupied, Allied troops rounded up all prisoners of war and registered everyone over the age of twelve. Nazi Party members were arrested. All able-bodied people were liable for rubble-clearing or burying the dead. As

Rebuilding Germany

the surrender had been unconditional, the German people had absolutely no political or civil rights. They were forbidden to write letters, use the telephone, travel more than four miles from home, or attend meetings. Food and medical supplies depended upon the whim of the individual Allied commander. Governing and running the whole of Germany down to village level was beyond the resources of the occupation forces. Military government teams therefore sought out those who had not been Nazis and appointed them to local government posts.

Konrad Adenauer's first period in office after the war was short. On 6 October 1945 he was dismissed by the British commandant of Cologne—Colonel Barraclough. The British had taken over from the Americans in Cologne, one of the most devastated cities in Europe. Colonel Barraclough accused Dr Adenauer of lacking energy in solving the problems of fuel and shelter in the city. This action was one of the most fortunate events in Konrad Adenauer's long life (1876–1967). Freed from his responsibilities in Cologne, Adenauer was able to throw himself vigorously into the work of rebuilding Germany's political life.

THE NEW PARTIES

Hitler had banned all political parties except his own National Socialists in 1933, but some managed to continue 'underground'. It was an important part of Allied policy to prepare Germany for democratic self-government. Four parties were licensed between June and December 1945. The Communist Party (K.P.D.) was the first to appear, quickly followed by the Social Democrats (S.P.D.). Adenauer had been a supporter of the Centre Party which had Roman Catholicism as its unifying force. By 1945 he had come to the conclusion that a broader-based party was needed, which would include all Christians who wanted a democratic rule in Germany. The Centre Party never revived successfully in its old form, but in the large cities the Christian Democratic Union (C.D.U.) arose and was the natural 'home' for Adenauer. With the powerful support of the Archbishop of Cologne, and the Protestant banker—Dr Pferdminges, Adenauer was elected chairman of the C.D.U. in the British Zone. His chief political rival was the Social Democrat, Dr Kurt Schumacher, a crippled survivor of Nazi concentration camps. In the Russian Zone, the K.P.D. swallowed up the S.P.D. and was unchallenged. In the Western zones the K.P.D. never achieved more than 8 per cent support.

DENAZIFICATION

One of the main tasks of the Allied Control Council was to destroy all traces of Nazism. This mainly involved hunting down former Nazis and preventing them from securing important positions under the occupation government. Those guilty of serious crimes would be put on trial.

The Russians made use of Nazis who would be valuable, such as rocket technicians; otherwise they were dismissed or transported to Siberia. To the French all Germans were Nazis but the British were unenthusiastic about 'denazification'. Only the Americans went about the task with energy and determination. Every German in their zone over the age of eighteen was obliged to fill in a detailed questionnaire of 131 questions. Eleven million forms were distributed and soon there were over 400 courts combing through them. Nearly a million arrests were made, resulting in 170,000 trials, more than four times as many as in all the other zones combined.

In October 1946 the Allies agreed upon a standard procedure for denazifying Germany, but by early 1948 the process had ended in all four zones apart from major war crime trials. The success of the programme is open to doubt if only because of the difficulty of taking action against seven million former Nazi Party members.

RE-EDUCATION

While attempting to root out at least all the major Nazis, the Allies began individual programmes to re-educate the Germans. This meant that they hoped to expose the evils of the Nazi régime and teach the German population the values of democratic government.

Teachers who had been Nazis were sacked which meant that there were often eighty children in a class. Textbooks which contained such references as 'dirty Jewish swindlers' had to be scrapped, and new ones provided. In their own zone, the French undertook this task with vigour and even built a new university at Mainz. The Americans provided youth clubs and 'America Houses' where young Germans could be politically re-educated whilst they enjoyed the recreation facilities. In the Russian Zone it appeared that a Nazi became re-educated simply by joining the Socialist Unity Party. The British seemed the least concerned about the past record of those they employed.

Free elections were introduced at village level—as early as January 1946 in the American Zone. Gradually larger elections were introduced with the Americans making the pace and the British following more cautiously. The French were much less concerned with this aspect and were accused of behaving like conquering lords. Probably the most dramatic aspect of the denazification programme was the series of trials of men and women accused of war crimes and crimes against humanity.

War Criminals

'A thousand years will pass and the guilt of Germany will not be erased'—Hans Frank

A deathly hush fell over the courtroom as the British Prosecutor—Sir Hartley Shawcross—read out the sworn statement of one Hermann Graebe:

'I walked round the mound and found myself confronted by an enormous grave. People were wedged closely together lying on top of each other with blood running over their shoulders from their heads. Some were still alive. The pit was already two-thirds full, about one thousand people. The man who did the shooting was an S.S. man. He had a tommy gun across his knees and was smoking a cigarette . . .'

This is an extract from the evidence which for ten months poured out of the German city of Nuremberg where twenty-one leading Nazis had been brought to trial. The trials opened in November 1945 and ended the following October. The accused came from all sections of the Nazi leadership—party bosses, Göring and Hess; Foreign Minister Ribbentrop; Governors of the conquered lands, Frank, Seyss-Inquart and

19

Judgment at Nuremberg

Rosenberg; slave master Saukel; the Jew-baiter Streicher; Gestapo chief Kaltenbrunner; military chiefs, Keitel, Jodl, Raeder and Dönitz; the banker Dr Schacht and others. One, Martin Bormann, was tried in his absence, and another, Robert Ley, committed suicide before the trials began.

The trial and punishment of a defeated enemy was not a new practice but it had not been customary in the west for many years. In his opening speech for the prosecution at Nuremberg, Sir Hartley Shawcross said: 'It is a fundamental part of these proceedings to establish for all time that international law has the power to declare that a war is criminal.'

The tribunal was composed of five members. The President was Lord Justice Lawrence and there was one judge from each of the four major victorious powers. Each judge had a deputy who could take over in case of illness or for another reason. The hearings lasted from 10 a.m. to 5 p.m. with an hour's break for lunch and two other short breaks. Each prisoner was provided with earphones through which he could hear a simultaneous translation of the proceedings. Each was defended by a competent German lawyer and his junior; the prosecution staff numbered over two thousand. When not in court, the prisoners were kept in solitary confinement and forbidden to talk to one another. They were allowed regular exercise in the courtyard of the prison, had a daily medical examination, and were fed on substantial if somewhat plain food. Göring lost over five stone during the trial.

Each day they were brought to the courtroom in groups of four, checked along the way by telephone. Once in court, they were put into the long dock under heavy guard. Spectators were searched every day for hidden weapons, by the American military policemen who lined the walls of the courtroom.

There was never any doubt about the guilt of most of the accused. Innumerable witnesses and masses of documents built up a damning case for the prosecution. After their opening speeches, the prosecutors called for the death sentence for all the accused, but nearly a year passed before the sentences were passed. The long trial imposed a considerable strain on all associated with it. The accused reacted in varying ways. Hess spent much of his time staring vacantly into space pretending to have lost his memory. Göring, proud of his position as No. 1 defendant, spent three days in the witness box and scored heavily against the American prosecutor. Speer spoke out with complete honesty, making no attempt to hide his guilt. Kaltenbrunner, the Gestapo chief, denied all the charges. Hans Fritzsche, head of German radio, sat dazedly in the dock wondering why he was there at all. When the verdicts were finally brought in, Fritzsche was acquitted, as were von Papen and Schacht. Seven received sentences ranging from ten years to life. The remaining eleven received the death sentence.

Two hours before the time of execution, Hermann Göring swallowed cyanide which had been smuggled into his cell. Soon after 1 a.m. on the morning of 16 October 1946, von Ribbentrop mounted the gallows followed at short intervals by Keitel, Kaltenbrunner, Rosenberg, Frank, Frick, Streicher, Seyss-Inquart, Sauckel and Jodl. The last named, you will recall, had called for generous treatment of the German people, after he had signed the surrender documents at Reims. The bodies were then cremated and the ashes dropped into the fast-flowing River Main.

THE CONDUCT OF THE TRIALS

While there was never any doubt about the guilt of the accused, the trials posed some awkward questions. If the Germans were guilty of aggressive war, then why weren't the Russian leaders in the dock, charged with attacking Poland and Finland in 1939? During the trials great emphasis was laid on the slaughter of the Jews. However, no one was permitted to mention the massacre of 10,000 Polish officers by the Russians at Katyn; nor could the defence draw attention to the Anglo-American destruction of Dresden, a helpless, undefended city packed with refugees. Charges of using slave labour were levelled at the German leaders, yet hundreds of thousands of Germans (P.O.W.s) were kept by the Allies long after the war. Many in the hands of the French and Russians were reduced to 'walking skeletons'.[1] Perhaps there is a grain of truth in Field-Marshal Montgomery's statement that Germany's real crime lay in waging an *unsuccessful* war.

OTHER TRIALS

Even before the Nuremberg trials began, the British had opened proceedings against Joseph Kramer, the Commandant of Belsen, and forty-four of his guards. During the postwar years, many similar trials have been held both inside and outside Germany. In November 1947 Otto Ohlendorf and three others were sentenced to death for the mass shooting of Jews. The following June, Doctors Gebhardt and Fischer were sentenced for their part in ghastly medical experiments on human guinea-pigs. Ilse Koch, known as the 'bitch of Buchenwald', received a life sentence for encouraging the murder of prisoners. Alfred Krupp, the industrialist, who had missed the Nuremberg Tribunal was brought to trial in July 1948 on charges of using slave labour. He was given twelve years and had all his property confiscated. After serving only three years, he was released, had his property restored and was one of Europe's richest men until his death in 1967.

Polish courts passed death sentences on Rudolf Höss, commandant of Auschwitz, and S.S. Brigadeführer Jurgen Stroop, who had destroyed the Warsaw ghetto in 1943. Each was hanged at the scene of his crime. The Czechs executed Max Rostock, commander of the S.S. detachment which had massacred the inhabitants of Lidice. In 1953 a French court passed sentences on S.S. men who had committed similar

[1] Eugene Davidson, *The Death and Life of Germany.*

22

butchery at Oradour in 1944. Karl Adolf Eichmann was picked up by Jewish agents in the Argentine in 1960. As former head of the Gestapo Jewish Resettlement Department, Eichmann was deeply implicated in the plan to exterminate Europe's Jews. After a long trial in Jerusalem he was hanged in 1962.

Former Nazis were also tried in German courts but there were many accusations of too lenient sentences. However, in 1956 thousands of P.O.W.s were released by the Russians. Many were able to offer important testimony in the war crimes trials and as a result a Central Office of Nazi Crimes was established at Ludwigsburg in 1958. Within five years it had secured over 5,000 convictions, and in 1963 initiated the trial of twenty S.S. guards from Auschwitz.

The Price of War

'*What about getting the Germans to pay for the damage?*'—J. Stalin, 1941

At Yalta and Potsdam, the Russians made it quite clear that they intended to extract as much as possible out of Germany in reparations. They had persuaded the Allies to allow them to take machinery, plant and manufactures out of Western zones in addition to what they could get from their own. In March 1946 the four powers reached agreement on the level of industrial capacity to be retained in Germany. It was decided that Germany could produce 50 per cent of the total she had achieved in 1938. Steel production was to be limited to 25 per cent. However, while the Western Allies were keeping their part of the Potsdam agreement—supplying plant to the Russians—the latter were not sending the required food and raw materials to the Western zones. In May, therefore, the British and Americans stopped the deliveries to the Russians. This created a food crisis in the Western zones. The daily ration barely exceeded 1,000 calories, about one-third of a normal adult's needs. It became necessary to spend millions of pounds to prevent mass starvation.

The French, like the Russians, had no interest in reviving

the German economy. The British found the strain of supporting their zone so great that they quickly accepted the American offer of economic integration. On 1 January 1947 the British and American Zones joined to form 'Bizonia' with the aim of making it self-supporting. Meanwhile, the Russians continued to strip their zone of everything of value. Great trainloads chugged eastwards until 1950. By this time Stalin admitted having taken reparations worth $3,600 million, but Western observers put the figure at five times this amount.

THE PEACE TREATIES

Following the decision at Potsdam, the Council of Foreign Ministers met at London in September 1945 to begin drafting Peace Treaties with the minor enemy powers—Italy, Finland, Hungary, Bulgaria and Rumania. Further meetings were held in Moscow, Paris and New York before the final terms were settled. They came into force on 15 September 1947.

The Terms

1. Each of the defeated powers had to pay reparation to the countries on whom they had inflicted damage:

Paid to:

	U.S.S.R. $	Yugoslavia $	Greece $	Czechoslovakia $	Albania $	Ethiopia $
Italy	100 million	125 million	105 million	—	5 million	25 million
Finland	300 million	—	—	—	—	—
Hungary	200 million	70 million	—	30 million	—	—
Bulgaria	—	25 million	45 million	—	—	—
Rumania	300 million	—	—	—	—	—

2. All five powers, except Bulgaria, lost territory. Italy lost all her overseas colonies. Finland and Rumania lost some areas on their frontiers to Russia, and there were other minor changes in Eastern Europe (see map on p. 25).

3. The armed forces of the defeated powers were reduced to a low level, which left Yugoslavia, under a Communist government, the strongest power in south-east Europe. Russia had pushed her western frontiers outwards along a thousand-mile front in addition to important gains from Japan in the Far East.

Frontier changes in Eastern Europe after 1946 Peace Treaties

AUSTRIA

'Four elephants in a canoe'—Dr Renner

Recognising that Austria had been more a victim than a partner of Nazi Germany, the Allies agreed in 1943 to re-establish a free and independent state as soon as possible. By the end of the war most of the country had been overrun by the Russians. They permitted the elderly socialist Dr Karl Renner to set up a provisional government consisting of

Dr Renner

members of the People's Party, the Socialists and the Communists. The Western Allies recognised the Renner Government in October 1945, after they had assured themselves that it had popular support. The new government embarked upon a vigorous campaign of spring cleaning. Democratic methods of government were brought back and all the laws passed by the Nazis were repealed. War criminals were hunted down and denazification carried out.[1] As in Germany, four occupation zones were established and the capital, Vienna, was also divided amongst the four Allies. For economic reasons the

[1] Morris West's novel *The Second Victory* gives an accurate and exciting account of postwar Austria.

The Occupation of Austria

country never became permanently divided although the Russians did not co-operate much. The four zones were interdependent. The Americans and Russians had most of the arable land whilst the British and French zones carried most of the livestock. The Russians controlled the oil wells and engineering works; the iron and steel works were in the British Zone, the French Zone contained valuable copper mines and most of the timber. It would have been very difficult in this situation to seal off the zones.

In November 1945 the first general election was held in which the Communists gained only four seats out of the 165. A coalition of the People's Party and the Socialists was set up and remained in office through several elections, until 1966. A draft peace treaty drawn up in July 1946 was rejected by the Russians. They claimed that the Nazis were secretly in control of Austria. In addition they demanded a share of £50 million of the Austrian wealth seized by Hitler in 1938. The rich flow of oil from the wells at Zistersdorf in their zone was probably the main reason why the Russians were in no hurry to leave. So Austria had to wait until 1955 before a peace treaty was signed and independence restored.

27

2   Europe Divided

The Cold War

'The Russians trust the United States more than they trust any power in the World'—Harry Hopkins, U.S. Secretary of State, 1945

Three Prime Ministers, Eden, Churchill and Attlee

THE END OF THE GRAND ALLIANCE

In the spring of 1946 the leader of His Majesty's Opposition, Winston Spencer Churchill, visited the United States. He was invited by President Truman to his home town of Fulton, to make his speech. For the first time in public, Churchill used a phrase which for months had cropped up in his private letters: 'From Stettin in the Baltic to Trieste in the Adriatic, an *iron curtain* has descended across the continent. Behind that line lie all the capitals of the states of central and eastern Europe—all are subject in one form or another not only to Soviet influence but to a very high and increasing measure of control from Moscow.'

He was drawing attention to the fact that, following the defeat of Germany, the U.S.S.R. now controlled Eastern Europe and much of the Balkans. The co-operation which had existed between Russia and the Western Allies had almost completely evaporated. During the two years following Germany's defeat it became clear that Europe was splitting into camps. The eastern half, dominated by Russia, and the western part, totally dependent upon the U.S.A. for its defence and for the money needed to make a recovery from the devastation of the war.

THE SUPER-POWERS

In 1914 politicians could speak of eight 'great powers' in the world. Six were European—Britain, France, Germany, Russia, Austria-Hungary and Italy, one Asian—Japan, and the United States of America. Austria-Hungary disappeared in 1918 and three powers were utterly defeated by 1945— Italy, Germany and Japan. France had been crushed by the Nazi occupation and swept by the tide of battle. Britain, having fought longer than any other power, was completely exhausted and could never hope to stand on equal terms with the two remaining great powers—America and Russia. The military and economic gap between these two powers and the former great powers has widened enormously since 1945. Neither Britain nor France fully understood this, both developing 'independent' nuclear forces. Since 1960 China has appeared as a giant in the East, becoming a nuclear power in 1964, but she is still far behind the two super-powers.

29

The 'Iron Curtain'

As the division of Europe hardened after 1945, the Western powers and Russia found themselves disagreeing ever more bitterly on a widening range of subjects. At first these quarrels were confined to fierce exchanges across conference tables, but in 1946 the first fighting took place between the two power blocs—the Greek Civil War. In 1948 the European struggle reached its height in Germany, and in 1950 became worldwide with the outbreak of the Korean War. This struggle between the Western powers and the Communist world is generally called the COLD WAR: 'cold' as distinct from a 'hot' or shooting war. Although many bullets and bombs have been expended, the two giants have taken great care to avoid becoming involved in an all-out war with each other. Such a war would bring in nuclear weapons and would mean the end of modern civilisation in the northern hemisphere of the world, at least.

Before 1914 the many great powers could never be certain who their possible enemies were. Secret diplomatic conferences took place regularly as each power sought to gain more friends. After 1945 the U.S.A. and Russia were the only two contestants left. Every move was regarded suspiciously by the other; every gain by one was a loss to the other; every political problem was tackled with the object of gaining an advantage. But although this situation did not show itself clearly until 1947, its roots went very deep.

THE ORIGINS OF THE COLD WAR

Although the Western powers and the Russians had appeared to work closely together during the war, there were many concealed arguments about military decisions and the future of Europe. The Grand Alliance had been formed because of the presence of a common enemy. When the war ended it was obvious that the Alliance would not survive.

From the earliest days of its existence the Communist state in Russia had been denounced and attacked by the Western powers. Help was sent to the anti-Communist forces during the Russian Civil War, 1918–20. The U.S.A. refused even to recognise the Communist Government until 1933. In 1939, with the Nazi threat becoming large, Chamberlain could still talk of having 'a profound mistrust of Russia'. Following the Russian attack on Finland later in 1939 the British and French nearly became involved in war with Russia as well as Germany. It needed Hitler's suicidal attack on Russia on 22 June 1941 for first the British and then the Americans to try to forget their hostility to Communism. Thus, the Grand Alliance was formed, but between 1945 and 1947 it crumbled, and from its ruins developed the Cold War.

THE FIRST QUARRELS

The Western leaders must have departed from the Potsdam Conference with heavy hearts. Over the central issue, Poland, they had received only worthless promises. Mikolajczyk, the leading Polish non-Communist, had his car lifted shoulder high by cheering crowds upon his return to Warsaw. But the native Communists, backed up by the secret police and Russian troops, set out to discredit him. Soon he had to flee the country. In Bulgaria the chief non-Communist, Petkov, was executed and his Rumanian opposite number, Maniu, was thrown into jail. The Hungarian—Ferenc Nagy, escaped by seeking refuge abroad. By 1947 the Russian grip on Eastern Europe was nearly complete and Greece seemed ready to fall into their lap. Churchill's fears expressed in 1945 and 1946 (see p. 29) seemed justified. Having gone to war with Hitler to rescue Poland, and later most of Europe, from the tentacles of Nazism, the Western leaders were dismayed to see half the Continent under the control of the Communists.

Apart from the reparations question, Truman and Attlee could feel happier about the German problem. Major agreements had been reached over administration but the problem eventually arose, what was to become of Germany? The Russians, who had suffered terribly during the war, were determined to keep Germany permanently weakened. The French, also victims of the German occupation, were close to the Russian point of view. In addition, both sought to extract as much as possible in reparations. With large populations to be fed in their zones, the British and Americans were more concerned about occupation costs. Their fusion of zones— Bizonia—as a preliminary measure towards making them self-supporting, naturally met with hostility from the Russians.

Relations between the Western Allies and Russia became steadily more icy and bitter. The latter saw the revival of West Germany as a huge Anglo-American plot to finish off what Hitler had failed to do. Germany, with its population of seventy million educated, skilled and energetic people, thus became the immediate centre of the struggle between the super-powers. The Russians would dearly have liked to advance to the Rhine, and talked of a four-power control of the Ruhr. The Americans regarded a strong and united Germany as a valuable addition to their strength, a bulwark against Communism. Up to 1947 the major quarrels had been between the British and Russians, while the Americans nursed the vain hope of withdrawing from Europe. But Britain was too weak to stand alone against Russia, so America was forced to step in.

The Greek Civil War

'*Hold Athens without bloodshed if possible . . . with bloodshed if necessary*'—Churchill, December 1944

THE TRUMAN DOCTRINE

On 12 March 1947, President Truman addressed both Houses of Congress in Washington. Here are some important extracts from his speech:

'Greece is not rich. During four years of occupation 1,000 villages have been burnt down. Eighty-eight per cent of the children have tuberculosis . . . the people are in desperate need of food, fuel and clothing. . . . I believe it must be the policy of the United States to support free peoples who are resisting attempted subjugation by armed minorities or by outside pressure. . . . If Greece should fall, confusion and disorder might well spread throughout the entire Middle East. The disappearance of Greece would have a profound effect upon those countries in Europe . . . which have struggled so long against overwhelming odds. . . . The free peoples of the world look to us for support in maintaining their freedoms. If we falter in our leadership we may endanger the peace of the world.'

He then asked Congress for $400 million to help Greece and Turkey.

This speech showed three highly important facts:

that the United States had finally abandoned her 150-year-old policy of 'isolationism',

that the United States was taking over the role of Britain as the strongest power in the Mediterranean and the Middle East,

that the United States did not feel that the United Nations Organization was capable of checking aggression in all circumstances, and was prepared to spend vast sums of money to contain (hold back) Communism.

You will have noticed that President Truman made several references to Greece in his speech. This country became the first arena in which the two super-powers struggled for supremacy.

THREE COLONELS

After the German invasion of Greece in April 1941, the government fled to Cairo. In Greece itself two resistance movements sprang up. The National Liberation Front (E.A.M. in Greek initials) and its National People's Liberation Army (E.L.A.S.) were Communist-led while the Greek Democratic National League (E.D.E.S.) was Nationalist and Republican. The Greek king-in-exile, George II, announced from Cairo that free elections would be held after the war. The two resistance groups did not want the king back unless the majority of the Greek people voted for him. On the advice of Churchill this was refused by the 'Cairo' government.

In 1944, judging that the Germans would soon be leaving Greece, E.L.A.S. attacked E.D.E.S. and was soon in control of the whole country apart from Athens. The German retreat began in October 1944. British troops were dispatched, but as the last Germans left Athens, all that stood between E.L.A.S. and the city were three British Colonels.

CIVIL WAR

E.A.M. had been promised six cabinet posts in the new government, which explains why they did not try to take over Athens. However, the new royal government could not rule efficiently while thousands of armed E.L.A.S. men were roaming the country. The government began trying to disarm E.L.A.S. The Communists moved into Athens and attacked the police stations. Soon British troops were drawn into the fighting and reinforcements were flown in. Churchill himself arrived in Greece on Christmas Day 1944 to arrange a settlement, and a truce was arranged for 11 January. Some leading Communists were executed, probably in revenge, after which the bulk of E.L.A.S. forces fled to Bulgaria and Yugoslavia.

A general election was held in March 1946 giving the royalists a popular vote of over 50 per cent and nearly 70 per cent voted for the return of the king. The Communist vote was very low and as a result the Greek government became the target for verbal attacks in the United Nations, and physical attacks from E.L.A.S. In the Security Council Greece was charged by the Communist bloc with threatening the peace of south-east Europe. Greece made countercharges and a U.N. Commission of Investigation was dispatched to make an on-the-spot enquiry. The report of the Commission eventually found in favour of Greece. In the meantime, the Greek government was being extremely hard-pressed by E.L.A.S. and had to call on Britain for help. It was estimated that Britain would need to spend £60 million in Greece during 1947 to save the government. This crisis came just at a time when Britain was in the grip of a very severe winter which was causing serious economic problems. It is quite possible that Stalin increased pressure on Greece because Britain was in such difficulties.

Ernest Bevin, the British Foreign Secretary, went to see the

Chancellor of the Exchequer, Hugh Dalton, to arrange for the money needed for Greece. 'If the Greeks want an army, they must pay for it themselves', said Dalton, and made it quite clear that there would be no more aid for Greece and Turkey after 31 March 1947. (Turkey was also being threatened by the Russians and was also receiving British aid.) Bevin immediately informed the American government of Britain's position. Thus it came about that on 12 March President Truman asked Congress for $400 million to help Greece and Turkey during the following fifteen months.

DEFEAT OF THE COMMUNISTS

The Americans poured hundreds of millions of dollars into Greece. The Army was re-equipped and industrial development carried out. This included the building of power stations, steel, cement and engineering works. Road and railway rebuilding was undertaken and efforts were made to modernise farming methods.

The civil war dragged on for three years. A quarrel in the Communist bloc, between Marshal Tito of Yugoslavia and

Soldiers of the Greek Army

Stalin, saved the Greek government. Perhaps as a snub to Stalin, Tito refused to allow E.L.A.S. men to retreat over his border. Stalin, probably because of other worries, seemed to lose interest in Greece. Thus by 1949 most of the Greek Communists were either taking refuge in Albania or had been imprisoned in Greece. If Greece had proved to be a failure for the Communists, they more than made up for it by a startling success in Central Europe.

Czechoslovakia

'Czechoslovakia is a truly democratic and socialist state'—President Beneš, 1947

A MYSTERIOUS DEATH

The Czechoslovak Foreign Minister was found dead in the courtyard of the Czernin Palace at 6.25 a.m. on 10 March 1948. Six hours later the government proclaimed he had committed suicide 'by jumping out of the window of his official apartment', and mentioned 'illness, insomnia and a moment of nervous disorder'.

But consider the following facts:

The head was undamaged, the eyes were closed and there were no bloodstains.

Several witnesses who crossed the courtyard only fifteen minutes before the body was found had not seen it. Yet a police doctor who made the first examination stated that death had occurred two hours before.

The window from which he was said to have jumped was small, narrow and high up the wall. Yet his bedroom window was large and accessible. In addition there was a gun and a case of assorted drugs at hand.

The post-mortem was carried out by a doctor who had worked for the Nazis while the deceased's own doctor was forbidden to attend.

'In either case whether Jan Masaryk [the name of the deceased Foreign Minister] was assassinated or committed suicide, his death brought it home to the world that the son of the founder and first President of the Czechoslovakian Republic could not live *unmolested* in Czechoslovak "People's Republic".'[1]

For Jan Masaryk's death took place only a fortnight after the Communist Party took over control of Czechoslovakia and added it to the Soviet bloc.

THE LEGACY OF MUNICH

In September 1938 Britain and France virtually surrendered Czechoslovakia to Hitler at the Munich Conference. Russia was not represented at Munich so no blame could be attached to her by the Czechs. The Western Allies, therefore, were regarded very unfavourably. After 1941 Stalin supported President Beneš's government-in-exile, the Czech National

Jan Masaryk and Dr Edward Beneš

[1] Otto Friedmann, *The Break-up of Czech Democracy*.

Committee in London. He also supported the proposed expulsion of Germans and Hungarians from Czechoslovak territory after the war. Finally, it was the Russians who liberated Czechoslovakia from the Nazi grip. Even though individual Russian soldiers behaved unpleasantly the Czechs were immensely grateful to Russia.

Thus it was not surprising that the Communist vote rose from 10 per cent in 1935 to 38 per cent in the first election held in May 1946. The Communists had become the strongest party in the country. They further consolidated their position by taking charge of the redistribution of land from those expelled (the *Volksdeutsche* and Hungarians).

Klement Gottwald, the Communist leader, became Prime Minister and appointed his supporters to the ministries of the Interior, Education, Information, Agriculture and Defence. The Deputy Foreign Minister was also a Communist. There was no opposition in Czechoslovakia after 1946. The five other active parties were welded into a National Front dominated by the Communists. The strongest prewar party, the Agrarians, were banned from fighting in elections.

As with the rest of Western Europe, Stalin encouraged the Czech Communists to secure complete control peaceably. But by mid-1947 it was obvious that American aid to Europe (see page 55) was going to prevent Communist takeovers. Stalin forbade the Czechs to accept American aid. As soon as this became generally known, anti-Communist feelings grew stronger. It became obvious that at the next election they would fall from power unless they did something drastic.

THE COMMUNIST TAKEOVER

The leaders of the democratic parties decided to expose the Communists. The Minister of the Interior, Nosek, had been systematically turning the police into a private (Communist) army. In February 1948 he dismissed the eight remaining non-Communist police commanders in Prague, and replaced them with Communists. Members of the government protested and when President Beneš refused to reinstate the police commanders, eight Ministers resigned. The legal result of this should have been a general election. Instead Beneš filled the eight vacancies with Communists.

In Prague 9,000 students held a protest march to Hradčany Castle to see the President. They were halted by a cordon of police and while the students hesitated more armed police arrived in cars. Suddenly the students began singing the national hymn and everyone including the police stood to attention! But when the singing had finished, the police opened fire. Three students were killed, 100 were wounded and 100 arrested.

After this there were no more public incidents. The Right Hon. R. H. S. Crossman, M.P., who was in Prague at the time, described the situation as 'a very quiet cold terror'. A new government was formed with a Communist majority. Four days later the former Minister of Justice was found under his window seriously injured, and ten days after that came the tragic death of Jan Masaryk. No doubt feeling that Czechoslovakia was no longer safe, eight important anti-Communist ex-ministers tried to flee the country. On 21 March they made their way to Rakovnick airport, forty miles north-west of Prague, but they were arrested by security police who reported seeing a foreign aircraft circling overhead.

Hubert Ripka, ex-Minister of Foreign Trade, was luckier. He evaded his 'shadow' by slipping out of the back of a friend's house while the front was being watched. For two days he hid in the forest close to Rakovnick airport, and managed to escape the police trap. He grew a beard and eventually escaped to France by train.

The Communist *coup d'état* (takeover) in Czechoslovakia marked the limit of Russia's advance into Europe. However, this success was one of the reasons why the Russians began to put pressure on another trouble-spot—Berlin.

West Germany

'*Perhaps fifty years will pass before Germans will understand democracy*'—General Koenig, 1946

THE LONDON CONFERENCE

At the time of the Czechoslovakian crisis a meeting was being held in London to consider the future of the three Western zones of Germany. The threat from Russia which seemed to hang over Europe made it necessary for the West to seek the support of the West Germans. At this conference, and a further one held in June 1948, it was decided to create a West German state with a strong, self-supporting economy. The new state was to be prepared for eventual independence.

The Russians who had refused an invitation to attend the London Conference were very annoyed at this decision. They accused the West of reviving Nazism and began to interfere with traffic between the Western zones and West Berlin. They also continued to turn their own zone into a one-party state, a plan which had begun in June 1947 and was complete by October 1949—the German Democratic Republic (D.D.R.).

The French were to be given the Saar, and the Ruhr was to be 'internationalised'. This meant that it would be placed under the control of a six-nation commission, Britain, France, Germany, Holland, Belgium and Luxemburg. These decisions were probably the price which America and Britain had to pay to gain France's support for the formation of a West German state.

CURRENCY REFORM

Of great importance was the decision to reform the Reichsmark—the German currency. Money had very little value in postwar Germany. It took a month's wages to buy a packet of American cigarettes—the real currency. A wealthy German was one who had cameras, binoculars, china, silver and jewellery which could be exchanged piece by piece for food on the black market. The ambition of most German girls seemed to be to marry an American or British soldier.

The Allies therefore decided that the first step in the rebuilding of Germany's economy must be to introduce a strong currency. This would put an end to the black market, check rising prices and encourage investments and savings. On 18 June 1948 West Germans began exchanging the old Reichsmark (RM) for the new Deutschmark (DM) at a rate of one for one for the first sixty. After that it was 1 DM for 10 RM. Many people suffered losses and much hardship as a result of these exchanges, but in the long run a firm base for Germany's economic recovery was provided.

U.S. military policemen searching for black market goods

The Russians refused to take part in the scheme unless they could print their own notes. The Allies refused to supply them with the plates for fear that they would print vast quantities deliberately to wreck the operation. To avoid trouble, therefore, the Western Allies did not introduce the DM into West Berlin. But on 21 June the Russians carried out their own currency reform and tried to force it into the Western zones of Berlin, so on 23 June the DM was introduced into West Berlin.

The following day the Russians carried out a most drastic retaliation upon the City.

The Berlin Airlift

'*Berlin will remain free; it will never become Communist*'—Franz Neumann, Chairman of the Berlin S.P.D.

A NEAR DISASTER

A file of children walked across the runway clutching their tiny bundles and climbed aboard the waiting Dakota. They had been waiting for several hours, and the watery winter sun was sinking fast as the motors revved. Lothar Zeidler, one of the older boys, looked out of the window as the plane headed north-west towards Lübeck. Below, he could see the silver band of the Elbe and at intervals the lights of the villages. For over an hour the flight proceeded smoothly, and then the passengers could feel the plane beginning to descend. The wireless operator came out of his cabin to warn them to fasten their safety belts. Everyone laughed at the funny sensations in their stomachs. Then the laughter changed to screams and shouts of alarm as something scraped along the bottom of the plane. Almost immediately the plane hit the ground, the lights went out and smoke filled the passenger compartment.

Lothar jumped up and was surprised to find himself uninjured. He struggled to open the door but it was jammed. Eventually, with the help of another passenger named Brandes, he forced it open. Outside he found a woman passenger lying under a broken window so he dragged her away from the now burning plane. Lothar helped injured passengers to scramble clear, then he found the pilot semiconscious and bleeding. He hauled him clear and tried to make him comfortable. By now the plane was burning fiercely and would explode any minute. The twenty-five survivors, most of them injured, struggled away to the edge of the forest for safety. Then Lothar and Brandes set off across the marshy countryside to find help. Nearly two hours later, soaked and exhausted, they reached a police station and the rescue operation began, with the help of Russian soldiers. For Dakota KP.491 had crashed in the Russian Zone of Germany. This aircraft was on one of 260,000 flights made to and from Berlin between 26 June 1948 and 12 May 1949. During this time the Russians were trying to force the Western Allies to leave Berlin by stopping all road, rail and canal transport to and from the city.

STEPS LEADING TO THE BLOCKADE

The first signs of trouble became visible three months before the Russians stopped land transport to West Berlin. On 20 March 1948 Marshal Sokolovsky walked out of the Allied Control Council following the decision of the Western powers to form a West German Republic. This was followed by a Russian demand to inspect all military trains passing through their zone. During April barges were held up and eight British convoys were delayed at the autobahn checkpoint. Then the Nord Express was cancelled. A much more serious

The Berlin Airlift, 1948–9

incident occurred on 5 June; when a Russian Mig fighter
'buzzed' and collided with a British Viking transport, killing
both crews. Early in June it was announced that the autobahn
bridge over the Elbe was being closed for 'repairs'. The currency reform on the 18th appeared to decide the Russians,
for they immediately stopped all east–west traffic. On the 21st
the last food train steamed into Berlin, and three days later the
blockade began.

THE AIR BRIDGE

General Clay, the American commander-in-chief in Germany,
promptly ordered all his transport aircraft to concentrate on
the Berlin route. On 26 June the U.S.A.A.F. brought in 80 tons

43

and the R.A.F. six-and-a-half. There were over two million people living in West Berlin and they now relied on the Western zones of Germany to supply all their food, fuel and clothing and raw materials by air. The Allied Commanders estimated that a daily minimum of 4,000 tons would be needed. General Clay thought that his aircraft could only manage 600 tons, but within three weeks the daily average was 1,200 and within three months 4,600 tons.

The U.S.A.A.F., which was handling about 70 per cent of the load, spared no effort to build up the airlift. Transport planes from U.S. bases in Japan, Hawaii, Alaska and Texas began to arrive in West Germany; C-47 Dakotas, C-54 Skymasters and then in mid-August the first C-74 Globemaster, capable of carrying a 20-ton load. By September planes were landing in Berlin at three-minute intervals day and night. An extra airstrip at Tegel in the French sector was built in two months by 20,000 German labourers working round the clock.

As the endless stream of huge transports poured down the air corridors to Berlin, the Russians did not remain idle. First they sought to win over the West Berliners by inviting them to register for extra rations in the Eastern Zone. Two per

The first 'Globemaster' being unloaded at Gatow

cent accepted! Then they established a firing range below one air-corridor and a bombing range below another on which they carried out repeated practices with live ammunition. Weather balloons were suspended in dangerous positions and false landing signals sent out. Buzzing incidents increased and on one occasion a squadron of Yaks swept over Gatow aerodrome 100 feet above the ground, performing a victory roll. Allied pilots were badly shaken by one encounter with a motley procession of Yaks, La-9s and Stormoviks streaming up the 'down' corridor. However, neither side was prepared to start a full-scale war over Berlin. The Russians stopped short of actually attacking Allied planes whilst the Western powers did not try to force an armoured column down the autobahn to break the blockade.

With the approach of winter, ice and fog were added to the list of troubles. Electricity supplies from the Eastern Zone had been cut off at the start of the blockade; this, added to a coal shortage, meant a most uncomfortable winter for West Berliners. Food rationing was strict but a great deal of smuggling took place at airports. One snap search of workers there revealed 129 tins of meat and two hundredweights of other foodstuffs.

In spite of these difficulties, the build-up continued. In February 1949 the daily average rose to 6,000 tons, and a month later to 8,000. Finally on 16 April 1949 the peak was reached. Throughout that day at an average interval of 62 seconds, 1,383 transports landed in Berlin, unloading 13,215 tons of supplies. At last the Russians realised that it was impossible to strangle West Berlin, and on 12 May the blockade was lifted. The airlift cost over £200 million.

The Two Germanys

'In rebuilding Germany, we want to learn from the mistakes of the past'—Konrad Adenauer

THE PARLIAMENTARY COUNCIL

If the Russians thought that the blockade of Berlin would change the Western Allies' plan for a Western German state, they were mistaken. Less than a week after the airlift began, the three Western military governors met at Frankfurt. They met at Frankfurt with the eleven Ministers President of the *länder* (states) of the Western zones to arrange for the summoning of an assembly or parliamentary council. This council was charged with the task of drawing up a democratic constitution for the new West German state. This democratic constitution is normally called the Basic Law.

Dr Adenauer at a C.D.U. rally

Konrad Adenauer was not at the Frankfurt conference, but as leader of the Christian Democratic Union (C.D.U.), he was at the first meeting of the parliamentary council. This was held on 1 September 1948 at the Teachers' College situated on the banks of the Rhine at Bonn. The C.D.U. and the S.P.D. had twenty-seven delegates each and there were eleven others including the Communists. Possibly because of the support of the non-Socialist groups, Adenauer was elected President of the Council.

THE BASIC LAW

The constitution-makers had to steer a careful path between creating a government that was too weak to rule effectively as during the Weimar Republic, and an all-powerful government as in the Third Reich. It was decided, therefore, to create a Federal Republic of eleven *länder* with two 'houses of parliament'—the Bundesrat and the Bundestag. The Bundesrat, the upper house, would represent the *länder*, and the Bundestag, the equivalent of the British House of Commons, would consist of popularly elected deputies. The Chancellor, unlike his Weimar predecessors, could not be dismissed unless the Bundestag could name a successor at the same time. The head of state was to be a President who, again, unlike the Weimar presidents, was to be elected by the two houses and not by popular vote. One further protection was the proposed establishment of a constitutional court similar to the Supreme Court of the U.S.A., to keep a watch on law-making.

THE FEDERAL REPUBLIC

The parliamentary council spent several months thrashing out the Basic Law. As President, Konrad Adenauer had the double task of ensuring a positive result, and of keeping the three military governors informed of all progress. The Allies complained of the time taken, but it was completed by April 1949 and came into force on 23 May. The three Western Allies each appointed a high commissioner who was responsible for foreign affairs, security, refugees and the Ruhr. Bonn became the Federal capital.

The first elections were held for the Bundestag on 14 August. Nearly 80 per cent of the electors cast their votes, giving the C.D.U. (139 seats) a slight majority over the S.P.D. (131 seats). The Free Democrats gained 52 seats and the remaining 80 were shared amongst the smaller parties. A month later Professor Theodor Heuss became the President and Konrad Adenauer the first Chancellor. Adenauer was elected by a majority of one vote and admitted having voted for himself! He then set about forming a coalition government composed of the C.D.U., F.D.P. and the German Party. The S.P.D. became the official opposition under the courageous Dr Schumacher who had recently had a leg amputated.

Within three weeks of the announcement of the Adenauer Government, the German Democratic Republic (D.D.R) was formed from the Eastern zone. Germany thus became completely and perhaps permanently divided into two directly opposed states.

3 Recovery and the Beginnings of Unity

U.N.R.R.A.

Following the defeat of Germany and her allies, the most immediate problem facing European nations was to repair the damage of war and restart industrial production. Foreseeing this task, the Allies—or United Nations, as they called themselves, established an organisation for the purpose of giving 'first aid' to the most devastated countries. This organisation, set up in November 1943, was called the United Nations Relief and Rehabilitation Administration, abbreviated to U.N.R.R.A. The driving forces behind U.N.R.R.A. were Dean Acheson, the American statesman, and Sir Frederick Leith Ross. The U.S.A. provided about two-thirds of the funds needed and Britain about one-sixth. Its staff, drawn from many nations, was a well-paid and mainly dedicated group, but U.N.R.R.A. was often accused of waste and inefficiency.

Operations began in the spring of 1944 and continued until June 1947. The first task was to provide food, clothing and medicines, then to provide equipment and money for the revival of agriculture. The final and most expensive task was the rebuilding and modernisation of transport systems and industry. Greece, Poland, Austria, Italy, Yugoslavia, Czechoslovakia and the Soviet Republics of White Russia and the Ukraine received the largest amounts. In Germany U.N.R.R.A. took care of refugees, but the civilian population was the responsibility of the military governments. During its three years of operation U.N.R.R.A. distributed twenty-two million tons of supplies and provided many million dollars-worth of aid.

When U.N.R.R.A. was disbanded, its work was taken over by the International Refugee Organisation (I.R.O.), the World Health Organisation (W.H.O.), the Food and Agri-

49

U.N.R.R.A. supplies

culture Organisation (F.A.O.) and the United Nations International Children's Emergency Fund (U.N.I.C.E.F.).

National Recovery, 1944–8

The damage in Europe was related to the fierceness of the fighting in each territory. France had been a savage battleground and nine months after its liberation was still 'undergoing emergency repairs'. The daily food ration in the cities was a little over 1,000 calories per person. Once the transport systems had been reorganised and the coal mines got working again, recovery was fairly quick. In 1947 Jean Monnet's plan for modernisation and equipment of French industry further speeded up recovery. Belgium and Norway found it necessary to carry out drastic currency reforms while both the latter country and Greece were severely handicapped by the loss of a great part of their merchant fleets. Greece soon had its railways working and most of its land being cultivated again. It was not possible to replace the merchant fleet until the Americans offered easy terms for the purchase of wartime 'liberty' ships. Denmark suffered least of all European countries from the German occupation, but found its economy hampered by trading difficulties in shattered Europe. As the only undefeated power in Western Europe, and one which helped greatly to destroy Nazism, Britain enjoyed tremendous respect and prestige in 1945. Probably no other power had fought so hard and given so much of its resources to winning the war. Thus in 1945 the British Government was in debt to the amount of £13,000 million, of which over a quarter was owed to foreign creditors. During the war years there had been a strict control on the production of consumer goods (clothes, furniture, etc). Wages had continued to rise so that in spite of income tax of 10s in the pound after 1940 there was a lot of money available for spending at the end of the war.

The Labour Government elected in July 1945 had two great programmes before it, both very expensive. First, it prepared to nationalise many great industries—coal, railways, gas, electricity and steel; secondly, it intended to develop the Welfare State, whose foundations had been laid by the Liberals before 1914. This meant the introduction of the National Health Service and various allowances and pensions for those in need. Britain was therefore in no state to enjoy any 'fruits of victory'. It soon became clear that a period of strict controls and rationing was necessary before Britain's economy would be soundly established. A massive loan of £1,000 million from the U.S.A. and Canada was soon swallowed up by a widening trade deficit (Britain was spending more abroad than she was earning). These difficulties were further increased by the terrible winter of early 1947 when traffic was paralysed, coal was in short supply and there were frequent power cuts. Factories were closed and soon two million men were out of work. It was at this time that Britain handed over her responsibilities in Greece to the U.S.A. By the end of 1947 the trade deficit was £600 million and when in 1948 there was little improvement, the Government was forced to take a drastic step. The pound was devalued. This meant that instead of being worth 4·03 dollars it was reduced to 2·80. This made British goods cheaper abroad and foreign goods dearer in Britain. There was a boom in exports and a decline in imports,

Stranded traffic on the Pennines, February 1947

so the economic situation improved for a while.

Holland was in a particularly difficult position. Before 1940 its prosperity flowed from two major sources—its empire in the East Indies and trade with Germany. During the war the East Indies had been overrun by the Japanese. They had set up an Indonesian Central Advisory Council under the chairmanship of Achmed Sukarno to pave the way for an Indonesian puppet state. Two days after the surrender of Japan in August 1945, Sukarno proclaimed the Indonesian Republic with himself as President. Although the Dutch Government fought in vain for three years to regain control of the empire, its vast natural wealth was lost to them. Many industries in Holland relied almost completely on the colonies. The question arose, how could the country survive without them? Even more vital to Holland was the future of Germany, which for years had been its greatest trading partner. Rotterdam, Holland's and now the world's greatest port, was primarily the port of the Ruhr. But the German occupation had left bitter memories in Holland.[1] There existed a love-hate relationship

[1] Even in 1966 the marriage of a Dutch princess to a German provoked demonstrations in Amsterdam.

52

between the two countries. An impoverished Germany meant an impoverished Holland, but a rich Germany spelt danger. Germany represented a vicious circle. The problem facing the Dutch was to 'square the circle'.

Economic Unity

'*Our policy is directed against hunger, poverty, despair and chaos*'— General George C. Marshall, U.S. Secretary of State, 1947

THE BENELUX UNION

Since that fateful day in May 1940 when the Luftwaffe had pulverised Rotterdam and the Panzers had overrun their defenceless land, the Dutch had seen one thing clearly: that neutrality, which in 1940 had meant keeping troops on the coast to prevent an English invasion, was a completely outdated idea. In September 1944, when German troops were still occupying their territories, representatives of the Dutch, Belgium and Luxembourg governments met to sign a customs convention. This meant that goods passing between the three states would eventually pay no duties. Goods entering from outside would pay a single rate of duty for all three countries. From this it was planned to allow the free movement of workers and capital, and develop a common policy in all money matters. By 1956, eight years after the customs union came into force, most of these plans had been fulfilled, and in 1960 full economic union was achieved.

THE EUROPEAN RECOVERY PROGRAMME

By early 1947, the situation in Europe had deteriorated considerably. The severe winter which paralysed Britain also affected north-west Europe and caused great suffering to populations already short of food, fuel, clothing and housing. In March a conference of foreign ministers held in Moscow ended in deadlock over Germany and Austria. Molotov continued to insist on $10,000 million in reparation and it proved impossible to agree over a fusion of all four zones. In the Balkans the British had reached the limit of their strength and handed over to the Americans. The Dutch were unable to trade their foodstuffs for the German coal which they desperately needed. In France, Italy and Czechoslovakia, Communist activity was increasingly menacing. European recovery was at a halt. The continent had become divided by the 'iron curtain' and the Western leaders felt sure that Stalin was taking advantage of the situation by trying to ferment Communist revolutions.

The American Secretary of State, General George C. Marshall, returned from the Moscow conference a very annoyed but determined man. He realised that the Russians would never agree to a prosperous Germany, which was necessary if Europe were to be revived. Even while he was in Moscow, his President had announced a step, the 'Truman

General George C. Marshall

Doctrine' (see p. 32), which was an exposure of British weakness. Marshall realised that with U.N.R.R.A. activities shortly coming to an end, Europe was still desperately short of capital, machinery and raw materials. Massive aid would be needed to revive the Continent and repair the damage of World War II.

In a famous speech at Harvard University in Massachusetts, on 5 June 1947, Marshall put forward his idea for a European Recovery Programme based on American aid. This is usually known as the Marshall Plan. There were these three essential points in the speech:

1. that there must be a request for aid from Europe (the U.S.A. had no intention of giving unwanted aid);
2. that the programme must be a joint American–European one and not a series of individual agreements between the U.S.A. and various European nations;
3. that the U.S.S.R. and the Communist states of Eastern Europe should be invited to participate, but the programme would go forward whether or not they joined in.

THE ORGANIZATION FOR EUROPEAN ECONOMIC CO-OPERATION (O.E.E.C.)

The British and French reacted enthusiastically to General Marshall's suggestions and arranged for a preliminary meeting in Paris in June 1947. Molotov, the Russian Foreign Minister, refused to join in a general programme. He insisted on a continuation of individual agreements with the U.S.A. Since the whole purpose of the Marshall Plan was to draw Europe closer together and revive trade, Molotov's suggestion was totally unacceptable to the West. The result was that not only did Russia refuse to participate, calling the Plan 'dollar imperialism', but they also forbade the Communist states of Eastern Europe to join. Czechoslovakia, still only semi-Communist, reacted violently to this order, as we saw on p. 38.

Fourteen nations met in Paris and drew up a joint report listing their needs and how they intended to use American aid. This report was submitted to President Truman and was approved by him and by Congress. During the first two-and-a-half years, no less than $12,000 million was provided, but no

American money was granted unless the receiving nation provided an equal amount. The Economic Co-operation Administration (E.C.A.) was established by the U.S. Government to ensure that all monies were spent only on approved recovery projects. In April 1948 a permanent European organisation, the O.E.E.C., was set up to administer the Recovery programme.

Although American generosity provided a massive boost to Europe's recovery, the O.E.E.C. was very limited. It was an international body. This means that the delegates represented their own countries' points of view. All decisions required a unanimous vote. The French were keen to introduce supranationalism. This means that the delegates would not be answerable to their own governments but would work for the general good of the Organisation. The British disliked supranationalism and, supported by the Scandinavians, they also opposed the formation of a customs union. Trade in Europe was obstructed by two obstacles; import duties which governments charged on foreign goods to protect home products, and quotas which prevented more than a certain amount of each product being imported. A customs union would sweep away all these artificial barriers and allow free trade between those nations taking part. Britain felt that tariff reductions and trade problems should be dealt with by G.A.T.T. (General Agreement on Tariffs and Trade), a body founded in 1947, and E.P.U. (European Payments Union), an offshoot of O.E.E.C. designed to make trading payments easier. With the formal ending of Marshall Aid in 1952 O.E.E.C. clearly began to decline in importance. Nevertheless an alternative plan to bring about closer economic and political co-operation in Europe had already been drawn up and was brought into operation at the beginning of 1953.

THE EUROPEAN COAL AND STEEL COMMUNITY
(E.C.S.C.)
Britain's opposition to economic supranationalism in Europe around 1949–50 had been successful but had run against the general feeling on the Continent. 'Isolationism' had saved Britain from Hitler's wrath in 1940. While the rest of Europe had known only defeat, occupation and humiliation, Britain

had gone through 'her finest hour'. When the war ended, the political systems of Germany, France and Italy had been thoroughly discredited. Smaller nations had been quick to realise that neutrality was no defence, and one result had been the Benelux Customs Union (see p. 53). Out of the ruin of Hitler's War emerged a strong feeling that a united Europe was the best hope for the Continent. The major question was who could give the lead. Britain, enjoying the highest prestige, clearly did not see herself as European. Germany and Italy, as defeated powers, could not. The Scandinavians supported Britain and the remaining powers were too small, except for France.

Two men in France fully understood the feelings in Europe and were not carried away by the paralysing fear of Germany which many of their colleagues felt. These two men were Robert Schuman (b. 1886) and Jean Monnet (b. 1888). Both were thoroughgoing internationalists. Schuman was born a

L to R: Dean Acheson, Ernest Bevin, Robert Schuman

German citizen and served as an officer in the German army in World War I. By the frontier changes of the Treaty of Versailles he became a French citizen and entered the National Assembly as a deputy for the Moselle. Monnet's family were in the wine trade and he travelled widely before and during World War I. He became Assistant Secretary-General of the League of Nations but was disappointed by the selfishness of members. Later he had business and financial dealings with China. Schuman was arrested by the Germans in 1940 but escaped to join the resistance. Monnet at this time was concerned with the purchasing and supply of equipment for the Free French Forces. Both men rose rapidly to prominence after World War II and were particularly concerned with economics and foreign affairs; Schuman as Minister of Finance, later as Prime Minister and then as Foreign Minister; Monnet in his role as organiser of a massive plan to modernise French industry. By 1949 Schuman could see that France's policy of trying to control West Germany was a failure since the Americans were more concerned with winning over the Germans than keeping them 'in chains'. He saw that a completely new approach to the German problem was needed. Monnet provided him with the answer: only by tying Germany economically and politically to the West could Franco-German rivalry be permanently ended. One major cause of this rivalry had been the mineral and industrial areas which lay close to their frontiers. If Europe's coal and steel industries could be brought under genuine supranational control, war between France and Germany would be impossible. This would then be a starting point, however limited, for an eventual European community. Monnet's plan was presented to the French Cabinet on 9 May 1950, only one day before a conference was due to start in London regarding the future of Germany. The plan was approved by the French. Dr Adenauer hailed it as 'a step of extraordinary importance for the peace of Europe', while the U.S. Secretary of State, Dean Acheson, called it 'so breath-taking that at first I did not grasp it'. The Italian Prime Minister, Alcide de Gasperi, was a man who shared Schuman's outlook, while the Benelux countries, pace-makers of European unity, welcomed the Schuman Plan, though Belgium had fears for her high-cost mines.

The great question mark hung over Britain, which in 1950 was producing half of Europe's coal and a third of her steel. The answer from Britain's Labour Government was not long in coming. While Britain welcomed the move to bring France and Germany closer together she could not accept a system which would hand over control of a vital part of her economy to a European authority. As neutrals, Sweden and Switzerland would not take part; Austria was partly under Russian control and Finland was closely bound to her by treaty. Denmark and Norway followed Britain while Portugal and Greece were too weak to join in a customs union. Neither Spain, which was thought to be Fascist by many, nor Yugoslavia, an independent Communist state, was invited to join. From June 1950 to March 1951 negotiations for the Schuman Plan took place between six nations—France, West Germany, Italy, Belgium, Holland and Luxembourg. These countries are generally referred to as 'the Six'.

THE ORGANISATION OF E.C.S.C.

Within the framework of E.C.S.C. are four major bodies. The first of these is the High Authority, which is the government of E.C.S.C. It has nine members, of whom not more than two may come from one country. It is completely independent of the governments of the member countries. The European civil servants who run E.C.S.C. do what is best for the Community and do not work for their own national interests. Attached to the High Authority is a Consultative Committee, representing producers, workers, consumers and dealers, which is consulted on all questions of policy.

The other three constituent bodies of E.C.S.C. provide the framework of a European political community. These were, first, the Common Assembly, now called the European Parliament. Its 142 members sit in political and not national groupings. By a two-thirds majority this body can compel the whole High Authority to resign. Second is the Council of Ministers through which individual governments express their opinions to the High Authority. Third, there is the Court of Justice which settles any disputes about decisions of the High Authority. It has seven judges and its decisions cannot be overruled or rejected by any national court.

Western Europe after Hitler

The European Parliament at Strasbourg

How the European Parliament works

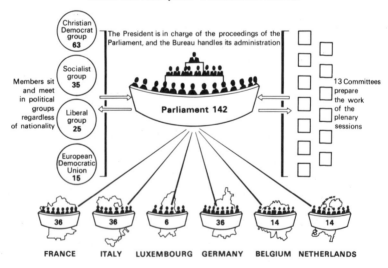

Christian Democrat group **63**

Socialist group **35**

Members sit and meet in political groups regardless of nationality

Liberal group **25**

European Democratic Union **15**

The President is in charge of the proceedings of the Parliament, and the Bureau handles its administration

Parliament 142

13 Committees prepare the work of the plenary sessions

FRANCE	ITALY	LUXEMBOURG	GERMANY	BELGIUM	NETHERLANDS
36	36	6	36	14	14

The national Parliaments nominate the 142 members of the European Parliament

The Treaties provide that the peoples of Europe shall in the near future elect their representatives direct

60

THE WORK OF E.C.S.C.

Since February 1953 member states of E.C.S.C. have been free to buy and sell coal, iron ore, steel and scrap unhindered by duties, quotas or privileges. During the first ten years trade in the above commodities increased amongst 'the Six' by 170 per cent. Prices showed only a 3 per cent rise compared with 24 per cent in the U.S.A. during this period. Money is provided for research and for expansion projects to firms within the community. All long-term planning has to be approved by the High Authority which also ensures competition by preventing unreasonable 'takeovers'.

It has been necessary to close old and expensively run mines due to the fall in demand for coal. Care has been taken to provide new jobs for the displaced miners (now 170,000) before the mines are closed. New factories producing rubber, aluminium, textiles, etc., have been set up in the worn-out coalfields. Some have been sent on retraining courses on full pay or moved to other coalfields. To make these movements less uncomfortable, the High Authority has also been responsible for the building of over 75,000 new houses and flats since 1954.

Coal and steel represented a very limited common market. E.C.S.C.'s most important role was to build the bridge to a full European Economic Community.

European steelworks

Political Unity

'*We must build a kind of United States of Europe*'—W. S.
Churchill, 1946

THE CONGRESS OF EUROPE

Economic unity is the first step to political unity. The idea of
binding the nations of Europe together under a common
government is a very old one. Some success had been achieved
by the Romans and by Napoleon and Hitler, but conquered
nations do not make willing partners. In fact, it was the frightful bloodshed and damage caused by Hitler which spurred on
the European movement. The 'Europeans' pointed out that
the vicious rivalry of the past, especially that between France
and Germany, was suicidal.

Churchill's famous speech at Zürich only fifteen months
after the end of World War II in Europe began the 'European' movement. 'The first step in the creation of the
European family must be a partnership between France and
Germany', he said. We have already seen how Monnet and
Schuman began applying this idea in the economic field. In
the political field organisations sprang up to seek European
unity. The United Europe Movement was founded in Britain
under the presidency of Churchill. A month later, in June
1947, the French Council for United Europe was set up.
Socialist groups formed the International Committee for the
Socialist United States of Europe. At the same time Count
Coudenhove-Kalergi, an Austrian who had suggested a
European federation in 1918, formed a European Parliamentary Union. Representatives from ten European parliaments
met to plan their campaign.

The 'Europeans' came together in a great congress held at
The Hague in 1948. Churchill, Adenauer, Schuman, De
Gasperi and many other famous politicians attended. Two
important resolutions were adopted. First, that the reconstruc-
tion of Europe must be done on a supranational, or at least
international basis. Second, that a European Union should be
launched, open to all democratic states in Europe which protected human rights. These were to be defined by charter and
protected by a European Court. The Congress rejected the

idea of a European Assembly to be elected by popular vote. They did agree that a Council of Europe should be formed from national Parliaments.

COUNCIL OF EUROPE

The Council of Europe was formed in May 1949 and now has eighteen members. Its headquarters are at Strasbourg in Eastern France close to the frontier with West Germany. It has two bodies, the Consultative Assembly which meets in public, and the Council of Ministers which meets in private. Defence matters are specifically excluded from the Council's discussions. Its main work is concerned with social and medical services, working conditions, education, travel and human rights. It seeks to develop a common approach amongst its members in dealing with these problems.

The Council has no power to enforce its decisions. Britain and the Scandinavian countries, the opponents of supra-nationalism, prevented the development of a true Parliament

Council of Europe representatives

of Europe. The Council has so far not been able to act as a springboard for political unity. Its value is as a meeting place for the exchange of opinion and ideas and for resolutions of solidarity amongst the member nations.

THE NORDIC COUNCIL

The Scandinavian countries—Norway, Denmark, Sweden, Iceland and Finland—strongly supported British opposition to supranationalism. Yet these countries have an excellent record of co-operation and unity dating back to the Middle Ages. For several hundred years there were only two great northern kingdoms, Norway–Denmark–Iceland in the west, and Sweden–Finland in the east. For 123 years (1397–1520), these two kingdoms were actually united under one crown. The pattern was broken in the early nineteenth century when Russia annexed Finland and the thrones of Norway and Sweden were united for ninety years. 'Scandinavianism' developed during the nineteenth century and during World War I Norway, Denmark and Sweden operated a form of trading group to avoid the effects of the Allied blockade and the German submarines. Finland and Iceland became independent in 1919 and all the five states formed the Norden Association to develop 'Scandinavianism'. There was also close co-operation in economic and foreign affairs. World War II split the five deeply, but the fault was not theirs and good relations were quickly established after 1945.

Only in defence matters are there differences. Norway, Denmark and Iceland are allies of the West. Sweden is neutral, while Finland is bound to Russia by treaty. The strongest ties are in similarity of language (except Finnish), culture and law. Since 1945 many organisations have been established to promote these ties, such as the Nordic Council of Fine Arts. Citizenship has tended to become 'Scandinavian' rather than national. For example, work permits have been abolished amongst the five and welfare allowances are payable (pensions after five years) to Scandinavians living in one of the five countries other than their homeland. Passports for travel between the five have been abolished since 1952. They have also operated a joint airline since 1946—Scandinavian Airlines System (S.A.S.). However, the greatest step forward came in 1952 with the formation of the Nordic (Scandinavian Parliamentary) Council.

The Nordic Council draws its representatives from national Parliaments but, unlike the Council of Europe, does not have separate Assemblies for delegates and Ministers. The Council deals with matters currently affecting two or more members, but has no power to enforce its decisions. Nevertheless, its decisions carry weight and have been acted upon by member governments. For example, criminals can be punished by the courts of other Scandinavian countries for offences committed in their own country. In 1954 the Nordic Council began debating the possibility of a Scandinavian Common Market. The Norwegians were not enthusiastic, but the problem became wider in 1957 with the Treaty of Rome, founding the European Common Market.

Military Unity

'Never in history have the principles of alliance been carried to such a pitch in time of peace'—Lord Ismay

THE DUNKIRK TREATY

Faced by the seeming threat of Russian military power (the Cold War), military unity came much more quickly to Western Europe than did either political or economic unity. The first step came in March 1947 with the signing of the Dunkirk Treaty by Britain and France. By this they cemented a fifty-year alliance supposedly aimed at countering the revival of German military aggression. The leaders of the two countries probably realised that Germany was no longer a danger but by naming her it avoided giving offence to the Russians. Within a year the Czechoslovakian takeover had changed attitudes in the West. A more general defensive treaty was signed, though Germany was again 'named'.

THE BRUSSELS TREATY

The two Dunkirk signatories were joined by the Benelux countries in a treaty signed at Brussels on 17 March 1948. The five nations agreed to build up a common defence system and a military committee under the direction of Field-Marshal B. L. Montgomery was formed. In addition, they undertook

65

to 'strengthen economic, social and cultural ties by which they are already united'.

Western Europe was still very weak economically and militarily at this time and would have been quite unable to meet a Russian attack alone. Only the U.S.A. possessed the necessary strength, and indeed the U.S. Government promised to help the Brussels powers to strengthen their defences. This was not enough to ensure the security of Western Europe as men like Ernest Bevin, the British Foreign Secretary, realised. He had only seen Brussels as a step forward to a much wider defence arrangement which would include all the great Western powers on both sides of the Atlantic. Louis St Laurent, the Canadian Prime Minister, and U.S. Senator Arthur Vandenberg, a senior Republican, strongly supported the idea. Vandenberg had been a fervent isolationist until Pearl Harbour. On 11 June 1948, as the Berlin crisis was boiling up, the American Senate passed by 64 votes to 4 Vandenberg's resolution that the Government should join any mutual defence agreement which would help the security of the U.S.A.

THE NORTH ATLANTIC TREATY ORGANISATION (N.A.T.O.)

The five 'Brussels' powers met with representatives of the U.S.A. and Canada at a conference in Washington at a time when the Berlin airlift was getting under way. This undoubtedly helped them to make up their minds. After three months of discussion it was recommended that a Western military alliance should be set up under a common commander-in-chief. The purpose would be to resist an attack upon themselves. In addition to the seven powers at Washington, Iceland, Norway, Denmark, Portugal and Italy were invited to join, and did so, but Sweden and Eire refused.

The North Atlantic Treaty was signed on 4 April 1949 in Washington. It called for the peaceful settlement of disputes, economic co-operation, the strengthening of military defence, the establishment of a N.A.T.O. Council and the admission of future members. The most important section came in Article 5: 'The Parties agree that an armed attack against one or more of them in Europe or North America, shall be considered as an attack against them *all*.'

A N.A.T.O. anniversary meeting

The Russians may have been impressed by this show of Western unity and strength although they denounced N.A.T.O. as an imperialist aggressive plot. Only a month after the signing of N.A.T.O., Stalin lifted the Berlin blockade. A little later, at the Congress of Foreign Ministers in Paris, some good progress was made on the problem of Germany, Berlin and an Austrian peace treaty. Then the Russians withdrew their support in Greece and the Communist rebellion collapsed. Stalin was not in full retreat; on the contrary, before the year's end he was able to announce triumphantly that Russia had become the world's second atomic power.

'*We are ready to bear arms once again*'—Dr Schuman, 1950

THE LAND OF THE MORNING CALM

Twelve thousand miles away from Europe, as the sun rose over the jagged mountains, a young couple walked away from their lonely farm. On his back, Kim Sang Mook carried a load of vegetables, eggs and poultry; his wife Lian carried their baby son. At the top of the first crest Kim and Lian turned to wave to their two other children, a boy of six and a girl of seven, who were looking after the farmhouse in their absence.

Kim and Lian sold their produce, bought some groceries and began their trek home in the late afternoon. Suddenly, the calm was broken by the roar of jet engines, the rat-tat-tat of machine-guns and a series of deafening explosions. Sick with dread, they hurried up the last hill and stared down the valley towards their home. All they could see was a heap of burning timbers from which rose a pall of black smoke. War had come to Korea and would cost the lives of three million of its inhabitants.

The kingdom of Korea had been the prize in a three-cornered struggle between China, Russia, and Japan in the nineteenth century. Japan gained control in 1910 but lost it upon her defeat in 1945. The south was occupied by American troops and the north by Russians. Both armies had left by 1949 leaving behind governments modelled on their own.

The Korean War began on 25 June 1950 when the army of the Communist north invaded the south. The Communist 'bloc' claimed that the south attacked first. News of the early fighting was flashed to Washington. Dean Acheson, U.S. Secretary of State, called for a meeting of the U.N. Security Council. In the absence of the Russian delegation, the Council recommended 'that the Members of the United Nations furnish such assistance to the Republic of (South) Korea as may be necessary to repel the armed attack and restore international peace and security in the area'.

United Nations troops (90 per cent of whom were American) began arriving in Korea. The North Koreans were driven back over their own frontiers and the U.N. advance reached almost to the Yalu River, the frontier of China. Only a year had passed since the successful Communist revolution in China. Probably fearing that the Americans might invade to destroy their revolution, the Chinese poured troops across the Yalu in November 1950. The so-called 'police action' of the U.N. rapidly became a hard-fought war.

THE EFFECTS OF KOREA

Although the fighting was confined to the 600-mile-long rugged peninsula where it began, the shock-waves from it

Turkish troops fighting in Korea

spread across the world. It led to general fear of a World War III. President Truman found it necessary to dismiss the American commander of the U.N. forces, General Douglas MacArthur, who wanted to extend the war into China by bombing supply lines. Amongst Asian nations, support for America rapidly declined as the war took on a 'White v. Yellow' aspect. At home, the Americans found themselves in the grip of a violent 'witch-hunt' led by Senator Joseph McCarthy, for Communists and sympathisers.

In Europe the founders of N.A.T.O. felt that they had only just been in time. However, N.A.T.O. had only fourteen divisions compared to an estimated 200 behind the 'Iron Curtain'. Fear of a European 'Korea' was strong. The Americans were now deeply involved in Korea and the French in Indo-China (Vietnam). Britain, like France, also had a rebellion on her hands in Malaya. Italy's armed forces were severely limited by the 1946 Peace Treaty. Thus it came about that only five years after the end of World War II, Western statesmen were discussing the possibility of filling the gap in Europe with West German troops.

THE EUROPEAN DEFENCE COMMUNITY (E.D.C.)

At a Council of Europe meeting in August 1950, Churchill proposed 'the immediate creation of a unified European

69

Army under the authority of a European Minister of Defence, subject to proper European democratic control and acting in full co-operation with the United States and Canada'. The British and French governments were opposed to a rapid West German rearmament. French public opinion, still vividly aware of the German occupation only six years before, was loud in its protests. The French were joined by all who had suffered at the hands of the Nazis, not least the Russians. The Americans, however, were becoming firm in their belief that German troops were the only possible answer to N.A.T.O.'s needs.

M. René Pleven

A possible solution to the problem was put forward by René Pleven, the French Prime Minister, in October 1950. He suggested the appointment of a European Defence Minister to a European Assembly; the formation of a European Defence Council with its own budget and the creation of a European Army including West Germans in mixed units. This meant that a European brigade might consist of a thousand French, a thousand Dutch and a thousand German troops under the command of a French General. The Pleven plan stressed that there should be no West German national army or Defence

Ministry. In spite of some doubts Adenauer supported it and so did Dr Schumacher, but his party, The S.P.D., did not. By a vote of 349 to 235 the French National Assembly accepted the plan to form a European Defence Community. A Treaty, broadly based on these lines, was drawn up and signed by the 'Six' in May 1952.

Britain remained as opposed to supranationalism in defence as she was in economics and politics. She still saw herself as the connecting link of three great circles—the North Atlantic, the European and her multiracial Commonwealth. Close support, but not complete integration, was to be her relationship with Europe. Even when the Conservatives, led by the 'European' Churchill, returned to office, there was no change of heart. 'All support short of membership' was his decision. The French and the Dutch were not prepared to put the E.D.C. Treaty into effect and face a rearmed Germany alone if Britain refused to join. In addition, the tension of 1950–2 began to slacken with the death of Stalin in March 1953. With the end of the Indo-China war in July 1954 the French were able to bring their army back to Europe and North Africa. After a long debate the French National Assembly finally threw out the E.D.C. Treaty. The Russians were jubilant, the Americans very annoyed and the West Germans worried for their future. Amidst this confusion a new plan was put forward by the British Foreign Secretary, Anthony Eden.

WEST GERMAN REARMAMENT AND INDEPENDENCE

At Eden's suggestion two conferences were called, in London and Paris in the autumn of 1954. Representatives of the U.S.A., Canada, Britain, France, Italy, West Germany and the Benelux countries were present. Their decisions, called the Paris Agreements, stated that West Germany should become a sovereign independent state and a member of N.A.T.O. on 5 May 1955. West Germany was to rearm, but *all* her forces were to be under N.A.T.O. command. N.A.T.O. forces would remain on German soil, Britain agreeing to maintain four divisions and a tactical Air Force on the Continent until 1998. West Germany and Italy were to sign the Brussels Treaty and join the five other signatories in the Western European Union.

The failure of the supranational E.D.C. and the triumph of

71

The Shah of Persia inspecting West German troops

internationalism in the Paris Agreements was a sad blow for the 'Europeans'. The limited success of E.C.S.C. and the integration of West Germany into the Western Alliance had solved one major problem. In addition, the Russians pulled out of Austria soon afterwards in return for a pledge of complete neutrality. Temporarily, however, the path to a United Europe had come to an end.

THE EUROPEAN UNITY MOVEMENT 1945-55

Economic	Political	Military
Benelux	Congress of Europe	Dunkirk Treaty
O.E.E.C.	Council of Europe	Brussels Treaty
E.C.S.C.	Nordic Council	N.A.T.O.
		W.E.U.
Limited success	Very limited success	Successful but failure of supranationalism

4　The Other Europe

The Thaw

'What will happen without me? The Country will perish because you do not know how to recognise enemies'—J. Stalin, 1953

A TIMELY DEATH

At 8 a.m. on 4 March 1953, a newsreader interrupted the music programme on Moscow Radio to make the following announcement:

'The Central Committee of the Communist Party of the Soviet Union and the Council of Ministers of the Soviet Union notify the misfortune which has overtaken our party and our people—the serious illness of Comrade J. V. Stalin.

'In the night of March 1st–2nd while in his Moscow apartment, Comrade Stalin suffered a cerebral haemorrhage affecting the vital areas of the brain. Comrade Stalin lost consciousness and paralysis of the right arm and leg set in. Loss of speech followed. There appeared to be serious disturbance in the functioning of the heart and breathing.

'The best medical brains have been summoned for Comrade Stalin's treatment under the guidance of the Minister of Health Dr A. F. Tretyakov together with L. I. Kuperin, Chief of the Medical Health Board of the Kremlin.'

All was in vain. Less than forty-eight hours later, the news was broadcast by the chief announcer Yuri Levitan that Stalin had died the previous evening, 5 March, at 9.50. Stalin, the man who 'found Russia working with a wooden plough and left her equipped with atomic piles', who for twenty-five years had ruled the Soviet Union with a hand of iron, was dead.

We do not know if Stalin's death was natural. Less than a fortnight before his death he was seen alive and well by the Indian Ambassador Mr Krishna Menon. He noticed that

Stalin was drawing wolves on a piece of paper with a red pencil. 'The Russian peasants know how to deal with wolves', he told Mr Menon, 'they have to be exterminated, but the wolves also know this and they will act accordingly.' It has been suggested[1] that the 'wolves' were Stalin's henchmen—Beria, Khrushchev, Mikoyan, Voroshilov and Bulganin, and that he was preparing to purge (kill off) a vast number of leading figures in the Soviet Union as he had done in the 1930s. To save their necks, it is said, Khrushchev and the others hatched a plot to poison Stalin and they succeeded.

L to R: Molotov, Voroshilov, Beria, Malenkov, Bulganin, Khrushchev, Kaganovich and Mikoyan flank Stalin's bier

STALIN'S STRANGLEHOLD

From the middle of 1944 much of Eastern Europe came under Soviet control. The limit was reached in 1948 with the Communist seizure of Czechoslovakia. Soon afterwards Yugoslavia was expelled from the Cominform for refusing to accept orders from Stalin. This meant that Yugoslavia was an outcast in the Communist world. During the next years Stalin introduced a number of measures into Eastern Europe to prevent any more 'Yugoslav-type' rebellions.

His first step was to root out and eliminate all 'national' Communists. At first arrest and imprisonment was enough—Patrascanu of Rumania and Gomulka of Poland being the first victims. In 1949 the purge intensified with the execution

[1] *The Death of Stalin*—'Monitor' (Wingate).

of Koçi Xoxe of Albania. He was followed by Rajk in Hungary, Kostov in Bulgaria and Clementis and Slansky in Czechoslovakia. Besides these major political figures many other minor party officials, army officers, educationalists and ordinary people were arrested. Some were executed, others sent to slave labour in Siberia.

Having crushed all possible opposition, Stalin decided that his own teaching would be the one true source of Communist ideas. These ideas would be preached through the Communist Information Bureau (Cominform). Next Stalin began tying the economies of Eastern Europe to that of the Soviet Union. This meant that each country had to produce according to the needs of Russia and not its own. Yugoslavia was subjected to a complete blockade. To carry out these economic policies, the Council for Mutual Economic Assistance (Comecon) was founded. No plans for co-operation were produced so each country continued its separate way. However, the rouble was fixed as the trading currency which was profitable to Russia. Trade with non-Communist countries was greatly reduced and that between Comecon members increased. In the military field, separate treaties were signed by the Soviet Union and each East European State. Strong units of the Red Army and Secret Police were stationed in each country.

Thus, by the time Stalin died in 1953, Eastern Europe was chained politically, militarily and economically to the Soviet Union. The name of Stalin was feared and hated by the native populations. To judge by the vast numbers who queued to see his embalmed body he was held in considerable affection by his own subjects.

COLLECTIVE LEADERSHIP

Stalin was mourned with due ceremony and his embalmed body placed next to that of Lenin in the Red Square Mausoleum in Moscow. Behind the scenes important changes were taking place. The Premiership went to Georgi M. Malenkov, and the First Secretaryship of the Communist Party to Nikita S. Khrushchev. The great Soviet war hero Marshal Zhukov was brought out of retirement to take command of the Red Army. This was to win the support of the Armed Forces in getting rid of the only man who might step into Stalin's

shoes—Lavrenti P. Beria. Under his command Beria had half
a million Security Police, highly trained, highly disciplined
and armed with the most modern weapons including tanks
and aeroplanes. During the confused hours following Stalin's
death Beria had not sought complete control although his
troops had sealed off Moscow. Nevertheless the other leaders
felt either he was a menace or that he should be made scape-
goat for Russia's troubles. In the summer of 1953 he was
arrested and his execution announced shortly before Christmas.

'They had had enough of dictators,' wrote Edward Crankshaw,[1] 'in the very earliest days following Stalin's death it was
already obvious that his successors were new men. They
smiled, they chatted, they mixed with the world . . . like men
out of prison . . . every one of them was determined that never
again would he have to submit to the tyranny which had lain
almost as heavily upon their lives as it had lain over the
breadth of suffering Russia.' In all their speeches and statements, the new leaders stressed that leadership would be
'collective', that they would rule jointly; none would have
precedence over the others.

The new leaders began introducing a number of highly
important changes, both in Russia itself and in their policy
towards other countries. They believed that Stalin's ideas
were made more in keeping with the 1930s than the 1950s.
From 1953 onwards it was possible to see a general thaw in
the Cold War. The Western nations and Russia have lost
much of their bitter hostility towards each other. The development of the hydrogen bomb and missile forces by both sides
showed that war was unthinkable. Therefore, they must learn
to live in peace together (coexistence). In Russia, the Secret
Police were stripped of much of their power, and political
prisoners were released from forced labour camps in Siberia.
Factories were ordered to produce more consumer goods and
luxury goods which had been scarce during Stalin's period.

The most immediate reaction came from outside Russia, in
the states of Eastern Europe overrun by the Red Army eight
years previously.

---

[1] E. Crankshaw, *Khrushchev's Russia*, Penguin (Special), 1959.

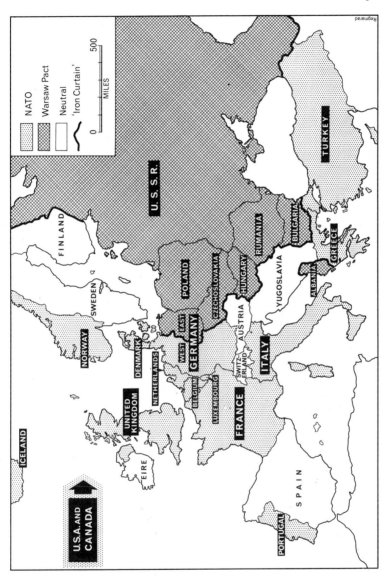

Military Divisions of Europe, 1955

THE EAST BERLIN UPRISING

The first sign of trouble began in Czechoslovakia. The Communist leader Klement Gottwald had died soon after returning from Stalin's funeral. Shortly afterwards a currency reform wiped out the workers' savings. Angered by their losses and spurred on by the evident weakness of their government the industrial workers of Pilsen protested. They organised a huge demonstration, took over the Town Hall and called on the government to resign. Troops were called in and the revolt died out.

Within a few days of the Pilsen incident, trouble broke out on an even greater scale in East Berlin (June 1953). It was sparked off in this case by a government order to increase production without extra pay. Street corner grumbles quickly developed into a massive revolt. On 17 June thousands of workers roamed the streets of East Berlin burning Soviet flags and pictures of Stalin and Ulbricht, the East German

East German Premier Walter Ulbricht

Premier. Other workers took over their factories. The riots spread like a forest fire through East Germany. The People's Police (Vopos) joined the rioters in some cities. Then the Red Army moved in and the unarmed workers found themselves helpless against tanks and machine-guns. Some 400 people died on the streets or later in front of firing squads. The latter included officers of the People's Police. The Communists put the blame for the revolt upon 'Fascists' from West Berlin.

The Soviet leaders realised that pressures were building up in Eastern Europe which must be released before they burst. Reforms were therefore introduced which became known as the 'New Course'. In Czechoslovakia, Poland and Hungary the 'police state' atmosphere lifted. More attention was paid to the production of consumer goods, which had been very scarce since the beginning of the war.

RUSSIA AND THE WORLD

The new Soviet leaders began to seek better relationships with the major powers of the world. In 1953 they withdrew claims to Turkish territory which they had made in 1945. Next came the Korean Armistice. It can be assumed that at the worst the Russians raised no objection—at the best they urged China to sign. In 1954 they played an important part as co-chairmen in the Indo-China Peace Conference (see p. 114). On 14 May 1955 they withdrew all objections to an Austrian Peace Treaty and signed the necessary documents.

The granting of independence and admission to N.A.T.O. of West Germany in May 1955 annoyed and probably worried the Russians. Their reply came a week later, the day before they signed the Austrian Peace Treaty. Representatives of the U.S.S.R., Poland, Rumania, Hungary, Czechoslovakia, Bulgaria and Albania met at Warsaw and signed a Military Pact. The Warsaw Pact, as it was known, placed all their armed forces under a single commander—the Soviet Marshal Koniev. In addition Soviet troops were given the legal right to be stationed in the countries of their fellow signatories.

At the end of the month (May 1955) Khrushchev and the Soviet Prime Minister, Nikolai Bulganin, flew to Belgrade to make their peace with Yugoslavia. Bulganin had replaced Malenkov in the previous February.

'I have only to shake my little finger and Tito will fall', Stalin once said. But for nearly seven years Tito had defied the ceaseless propaganda, the economic blockade and the threats of rebellion and assassination. Now Khrushchev and Bulganin were coming to admit the failure of the Stalin policy and seek better relations with President Tito. The visit also gave Western observers the chance to see at first hand the man who was to rule the Soviet Union until October 1964.

On arrival at Belgrade airport, Khrushchev, dressed in a grey sacklike suit, bounded down the aeroplane steps to greet Tito. The Yugoslav President by contrast wore a magnificent

Marshal Tito and Mr Khrushchev meet at Belgrade, 1955

uniform and had arrived in a gleaming Rolls-Royce. Khrushchev then made a long speech putting all the blame for the Russo-Yugoslav dispute upon Beria, the late unlamented Soviet police chief. During his visit Khrushchev also showed a fondness for strong drink which led to some undignified behaviour. Nevertheless, the main purpose of the visit, the recognition of Yugoslavia as a true Communist state, was achieved.

Six months later 'B and K', as they were now known in the West, visited India where they were received with enormous enthusiasm. Khrushchev said that during their 200-year-rule there the British had been 'robbers in the full sense of the word'. He also accused the three Western powers of encouraging the Nazi invasion of Russia in 1941.

Their low opinion of the British did not stop the two leaders arriving in London in April 1956, where they were promptly nicknamed 'Bulge and Crush'. Their reception was polite but cool. The only sensation came at a meeting with the Labour

Mr Khrushchev entering No. 10 Downing St., May 1956

Party leaders, then in opposition. When the fate of certain East European socialists came up, Khrushchev clashed sharply with George Brown (Foreign Secretary 1966–1968). The Soviet leader said that if he lived in England he would be a Conservative.

After their return to Moscow, Khrushchev and Bulganin received a return visit from Tito to consolidate their new-found friendship. By the summer of 1956 Khrushchev was a world-famous figure and held in much higher regard than either Lenin or Stalin had been. Relations with the West appeared to have improved considerably. As in 1953 the Soviet leaders suddenly found that it was from the Eastern European states that the greatest threat came.

The Year of Revolutions

'*The path of socialist development differs in various countries*'—
Khrushchev–Tito declaration, 1955

KHRUSHCHEV'S SECRET SPEECH

In February 1956, before his visit to Britain, Khrushchev attended the Twentieth Congress of the Soviet Communist Party in Moscow. Every leading government and party official was present as well as delegates from all the Communist Parties of the world. In his opening speech Khrushchev put forward the new ideas of the Party. He said that the Communist countries and the Western capitalist powers could live in peace together and that war was not inevitable. Not surprisingly, in view of the developments over Yugoslavia, he said that Communist states did not have slavishly to follow Russia's pattern of political and economic development. It was noticed that he made few references to Stalin in this speech and even fewer statements of praise. Delegates also noticed that Stalin's portrait was absent from the hall.

The first major sensation of the Congress came on the third day when Anastas Mikoyan, former Soviet Minister for Foreign Trade, rose to speak. He said that for the last twenty years of Stalin's life there had been no collective leadership and described how Stalin had been built and built himself up into a demi-god. Then he went on to attack Stalin's economic policies. It was clear to the assembled delegates that the Party leaders had been privately attacking Stalin for some time. The greatest sensation of the Congress came at the final session, which lasted from the afternoon of Friday 24 February 1956 to 2 p.m. the following day. Delegates began to expect something unusual when they were told shortly before the session that it would be closed to all except Soviet Communists. The Friday afternoon was taken up by a speech by Khrushchev lasting three hours. He systematically destroyed the image, built up over many years, of Stalin as the heir of Lenin, the Father of his people and the saviour of his country. As the speech unfolded, delegates listened, probably astonished and upset, at three major charges against the late leader. First, Khrushchev accused him of mass murder of innocent party members and government officials dating back to the 1930s. Next came an attack on Stalin's reputation as a war leader. Having ignored the warnings of Hitler's impending attack in June 1941, he said, Stalin had handled his forces in such a way that losses were astronomical in the first year. In spite of the damage he had done to the Red Army, Khrushchev continued, Stalin ordered the production of books and films glorifying himself as a military genius. 'They made us feel sick', he said, and then began to develop his third charge—Stalin's self-glorification. By the time Khrushchev had finished, he had turned Stalin from a kindly genius into a monster of terror and tyranny. It was small wonder that an Italian Communist watching the delegates emerge thought that they looked 'terribly upset'.

Although Khrushchev actually delivered the speech he must have made it with the full knowledge and consent of the Soviet leaders. It showed an obvious desire to break from the Stalinist past. It was also taking a tremendous risk since it attacked the Party itself, the fount of all authority in the Communist world. Finally, the long-term effects of the speech could not be gauged. 'The Chinese would certainly not like it'. Khrushchev was obviously a courageous and self-confident man. If his speech failed to gain the necessary support in the Soviet Union and abroad, it could be that on that cold February afternoon Khrushchev had built his own gallows: 1956 was to provide the test.

REBELLION IN POLAND

'*We have shed our blood to liberate this country and now you want to hand it over to the Americans*'—Khrushchev to Polish leaders, 1956

Numbered copies of a shortened version of Khrushchev's speech were circulated to Communist Party Branches in the Soviet Union with strict instructions that they were to be returned to Moscow after being read. One copy fell into the hands of American intelligence agents who dispatched a translation to Washington. After leaking extracts to the press, the Americans published it in full on 2 June 1956. Shortly afterwards, Tito visited Moscow and was fully accepted as the leader of an independent Communist state. For several years the world's Communist Parties had been taught to regard Stalin as the fountain of all truth and goodness whilst Tito was the arch-enemy. Suddenly, their roles were reversed and loyal party members found it terribly confusing. In Eastern Europe, envy of Yugoslavia's privileged position combined with anti-Stalinist feelings to make an explosive situation.

The first outbreak of trouble came in the Polish city of Poznan on 27 June. Workers from the large engineering factory there sent a deputation to Warsaw to protest about wages and working conditions. A rumour of their arrest led to a massive demonstration in the main square of Poznan, watched by hundreds of Western businessmen attending the Trade Fair. Security police opened fire on the crowd, who returned it with weapons given by sympathetic soldiers of the Polish Army. By the time order was restored, fifty people were dead.

After first putting the blame for the riots on 'Fascists', 'Imperialists' and 'American agents', the Government drew attention to the miserable living standards of most workers. A Russian delegation led by Bulganin quickly arrived in Warsaw and offered £10 million-worth of consumer goods. It was too little and too late. The mood of rebellion had already spread to the Polish leadership.

Poland's leading Stalinist—Boleslaw Beirut—had died soon after the Twentieth Party Congress. 'The truth killed him', said some. Other Stalinists were pressed to resign. For leadership, the rest turned to Wladyslaw Gomulka, imprisoned by

Stalin in 1948 but returned to favour in 1956. Gomulka wanted 'national Communism', that is an end to Russian domination and an end to the Stalinist tyranny in Polish life and politics.

The Poles secured strange allies—the Chinese. The leading Polish Communists decided in October 1956 to elect Gomulka to the post of First Secretary of the Polish Communist Party. They also resolved to exclude from the Committee the Soviet Marshal Konstantin Rokossovsky and three remaining Stalinists. Although born in Poland, Rokossovsky had become a Soviet citizen and was appointed Polish Defence Minister by Stalin in 1949. The move to shut him out of the Party

L to R: Marshal Rokossovsky, F.-M. Montgomery, Marshal Zhukov

Committee was a direct challenge to Russian authority. The Stalinists thereupon plotted to regain power with the Russian-commanded Polish Army. They were thwarted by workers from the Zeran car factory who used their vehicles to keep a watch for suspicious troop movements. If it had come to the choice, the Polish troops would most probably have remained loyal to Gomulka.

Moscow was now getting worried, and, without warning,

Khrushchev, Molotov and other Soviet leaders landed in Warsaw. Simultaneously, units of the Red Army began advancing on the capital. The Polish leaders hurriedly broke up their meeting and drove out to the airport to meet their unexpected and unwelcome visitors. The Polish leaders pointed out that they were not seeking to leave the Soviet bloc. They wanted independence similar to Yugoslavia's and an end to all Stalinist policies. They also wanted Gomulka to be Prime Minister and First Secretary and told the Russians that they would fight if necessary. Whilst the Red Army was overwhelmingly stronger, the Soviet leaders recognised the fighting qualities of the Poles. There was the additional danger that the shooting might spread into East Germany and other nearby states, possibly even provoking Western intervention. Accordingly, Khrushchev agreed to Gomulka's terms and flew home. Gomulka and his colleagues became popular heroes and Rokossovsky failed to gain election to the Party Committee. The following day, 23 October, his deputy, General Witaszewski, was dismissed. By then the eyes of the world had turned south—to Hungary.

THE BATTLE AT THE RADIO STATION

'*We should have crushed them* [*the Poles*] *like flies*'—Marshal Zhukov.

From all parts of Budapest the marchers came. In almost complete silence they headed towards the statue of Sándor Petőfi, the nineteenth-century hero of Hungary who died fighting the Czarist troops. Some held Polish flags to show their support for their neighbours in their bloodless fight with the Russians. After laying wreaths and listening to speeches at the Petőfi statue, they headed towards that of Joseph Bem, the Polish general who had fought alongside Petőfi.

On the long march to Bem's statue, the demonstrators began to find voice. Inspired by recent events in Poland, they called for Polish–Hungarian friendship, for an end to Stalinism and for the election of Hungary's 'Gomulka'—Imre Nagy. Most insistently they shouted 'Russians go home!' Bem Square was overlooked by Hungarian army barracks. Off-duty soldiers waved encouragingly to the marchers entering the Square, showing with whom they would side in the event of trouble.

While the main groups of demonstrators marched to the Parliament Building and heard a speech from Nagy, younger members headed for the Radio Budapest Building. They demanded the broadcasting of their sixteen-point programme but were refused permission. This programme included the evacuation of Russian troops, the end of Stalinism, economic changes to improve living standards and political freedom. While the students argued with the Radio director, A.V.O. (security police) men began to arrive. Everyone broke off at 8.00 p.m. to listen to a broadcast by Communist Party Secretary Erno Gerö. In a disastrous speech he failed completely to understand the mood of the people, calling them 'trouble-makers' and 'hostile elements'. After listening in shocked silence, the demonstrators began an organised attack on the Radio Station. One group of youths began reversing a car into the main gates while others clambered onto the balconies. The defenders used tear gas and fire hoses. When these failed, the A.V.O. began advancing with fixed bayonets. At about 9.00 p.m. the first shots were fired killing a girl of fourteen. The battle began in earnest. Tanks and machine-guns joined in, and soon the streets were littered with dead and wounded.

Some youths headed for the City Park where they tied steel cables around the huge statue of Stalin and hooked them to a heavy lorry. With an enormous crash the statue broke off at the boots and was later dragged through the streets by a refuse truck. By early morning fighting had spread throughout the city. The Central Committee of the Hungarian Communist Party was split between the 'Stalinists' who wanted to call in Russian troops and the moderates led by Nagy, who wanted a 'national' solution.

THE DEPARTURE OF THE RUSSIANS

The next morning, 24 October 1956, Nagy was named Prime Minister of Hungary and decreed the death penalty for 'trouble-makers'. Meanwhile, the Radio announced that 'Government *organisations* have called for help from Soviet troops stationed in Hungary . . . Soviet troops will help in the restoration of order'.

So Russian troops and tanks came into Budapest but most

The toppled statue of Stalin

of the Hungarian Army joined the rebels. By all the rules of war, the Russians should quickly have gained the upper hand. Advised by experienced officers, the young freedom fighters quickly learned the best way of dealing with Russian tanks: as a column entered a narrow street, the Hungarians attacked the first and last tanks with petrol bombs. The remainder were then trapped between the immobilised vehicles. The only Hungarian allies of the Russians were the A.V.O. They were shown no mercy by the freedom fighters. One badly wounded A.V.O. man was dragged from a hospital bed, kicked to death and hanged by his ankles from a nearby tree. Others were shot down as they emerged from their captured headquarters. After five days, the Russian forces found that they were too weak to put down the revolution and began to evacuate Budapest. By 31 October the capital was clear of Russians.

Nagy, meanwhile, had formed a new government composed not only of Communists but also members of the former Old

Socialist and Peasant Parties. He then announced a policy which went much further than the Poles had. He proposed that Hungary should leave the Warsaw Pact and Comecon and become a neutral, independent state such as Austria had been since May 1955.

THE RETURN OF THE RUSSIANS

Nagy must have known that the Russians would never agree to any change in Hungary's status. The example could lead to similar demands in Poland and Czechoslovakia. Communist leaders, including the Chinese, strongly advised Khrushchev to move against Hungary. Other factors influenced him. First the world was already in turmoil over the Suez crisis. In the early days of November, Britain, France and Israel launched

Daily Mail MORNING SPECIAL

NO. 18,826 TWOPENCE · FOR QUEEN AND COMMONWEALTH · SATURDAY, OCTOBER 27, 1956

BARBER BRINGS OUT THE FIRST REPORT FROM HUNGAR

'At least 1,000 have been killed in the most ghastly massacre. It was cold-blooded murder. But the Soviets have only stiffened and angered the people.'

I SEE BUDAPEST DYING

Tanks and artillery mow down cheering crowd

ARMOURED CARS FIRE AT ALL

THIS IS THE PICTURE BARBER TOOK WITH HIS OWN CAMERA

From NOEL BARBER: Budapest, Friday

...GHT Budapest is a city that is slowly ...ring. Black flags hang from every window. ...ing the past four days thousands of its citizens fighting to throw off the yoke of Russia have been killed or wounded.

'PUSKAS DIES FIGHTING'

DAILY MAIL: FLEET ST.

a co-ordinated attack on Egypt (see p. 121) and split the Western world. Any firm action by the Americans over Hungary was rendered even more unlikely by the forthcoming Presidential election. Finally, Khrushchev's own position in the Soviet ruling group was unsure. Any weakness over Hungary would have brought about his downfall.

At 5.20 a.m. on Sunday 4 November Imre Nagy broadcast on Radio Budapest. 'Today at dawn strong Soviet forces launched an attack against the capital with the obvious purpose of overthrowing the legal Hungarian Government. Our troops are fighting, the Government is at its post. I notify the people of our country and of the entire world of these facts.' Six thousand Russian tanks, too heavy to be knocked out by petrol bombs, took part in the attack. The fighting was short but very bitter. Nagy and his friends took refuge in the Yugoslav Embassy and a pro-Soviet Government led by János Kádár established itself. Nearly 200,000 Hungarians fled westwards over the Austrian frontier.

After the fighting, a general strike lingered on for several days, but slowly normality returned. With heavy hearts the Hungarians set about burying the dead and repairing the devastated capital.

The final tragedy came eighteen months later. Tricked out of the Yugoslav Embassy by promise of a safe conduct, Nagy and his associates had been arrested in November 1956. After a long stay in prison they were brought to trial in Budapest. The execution of Imre Nagy was announced on 17 June 1958.

The Khrushchev Age

KHRUSHCHEV IN COMMAND

The successful crushing of the Hungarian uprising did not end Khrushchev's troubles at home. At an important Party meeting in December 1956 a State Economic Commission was established, against Khrushchev's wishes, to run the Soviet economy. During the following six weeks Khrushchev gathered supporters, including the Chinese Foreign Minister, Chou En-Lai, and secured the reversal of the December meeting.

By the middle of 1957 Khrushchev's position was still in the balance. It is thought that a movement was afoot to have him dismissed from the post of Party Secretary. Khrushchev hit back by demanding that all differences should be thrashed out at a full meeting of the Central Committee. Marshal Zhukov, who had been humiliated by Stalin after the war, came to Khrushchev's aid. He provided army aeroplanes to bring Committee members from remoter parts of the U.S.S.R. These were mainly Khrushchev men. At a crowded meeting on 22 June no fewer than 215 delegates requested to speak.

At first, Khrushchev was on the defensive. Malenkov, Molotov and Kaganovich attacked him for his economic policies and for wanting to end collective leadership. Then his supporters from the provinces rallied to his side and when the final count was taken Khrushchev emerged triumphant. Four months later he sacked Marshal Zhukov from the Ministry of Defence. Since the death of Stalin and the 'shackling' of the security police, the Army appeared to be playing an increasingly important part in Soviet affairs. Khrushchev was determined to end this trend. Only one man now stood between him and the highest powers in the State, Prime Minister Nikolai A. Bulganin. In March 1958, when elections to the Supreme Soviet took place, Bulganin's formal resignation was announced. Instead of proposing Bulganin's re-election, President Voroshilov said: 'On behalf of the Central Committee of the Communist Party of the Soviet Union, I propose Comrade Nikita Sergeyevich Khrushchev as chairman of the Council of Ministers of the U.S.S.R.' This brought delegates to their feet in a prolonged burst of cheering. Collective leadership, for the time being, had come to an end.

Unlike Stalin, Khrushchev was generous to his ex-opponents. Molotov was appointed ambassador to Outer Mongolia and Malenkov to manage a power station in Kazakhstan. Bulganin became chairman of the State Bank and Marshal Zhukov was eventually pensioned off.

PEACEFUL COEXISTENCE

'A great deal depends on the understanding between our two states' —
Khrushchev to U.S. journalists, 1957

On 4 October 1957 the Soviet Union launched the world's

first artificial satellite—Sputnik 1. It was less than two feet in diameter and circled the earth once every one-and-a-half hours. This success showed that in certain fields of science and technology the U.S.S.R. led the world, including the mighty U.S.A. Nobody was more shocked and shaken than the Americans, who for decades had taken their lead for granted. Three months later they hurriedly launched a much smaller satellite of their own. The Russians remained well ahead, eventually putting the first man into orbit—Major Yuri Gagarin. All these space flights were launched by gigantic rockets. As the two super-powers raced to gain the lead in the development of these missiles, a new realisation began to grow in the minds of statemen. Against these high-velocity missiles, each carrying more destruction than all the bombs of World War II, there was no defence. There could be no 'winner' in in an all-out war involving nuclear weapons. The nations of the world must exist together in peace. As the Labour Prime Minister of Britain, Clement Attlee, once said, 'The alternative to coexistence is co-death.'

It was not until six years after Sputnik 1 that this realisation took the form of positive action—the partial Nuclear Test Ban Treaty. Meanwhile, Khrushchev began to probe an old trouble spot—Berlin.

GERMANY AND BERLIN

For nearly ten years after the end of the blockade (May 1949), West Berlin remained untouched by the world's troubles. Even during the East Berlin uprising of June 1953 police and Allied troops prevented West Berliners from joining in the fighting. The two halves of the city grew up separately. The Western half received lavish American aid and made an important contribution to the booming West German economy. In the Eastern half economic progress was slower. Theatres, cinemas and departmental stores in the West attracted thousands of visitors from the Eastern sector. More worrying to the East German Government was the constant emigration of its citizens to the West, about a quarter of a million per year. This loss of young skilled men was undoubtedly one reason why Khrushchev sought to gain control of traffic leaving West Berlin. In November 1958 the Soviet

leader told the three Western powers that they had six months
to accept his new proposals for Germany and Berlin. First,
they must recognise the East German State (D.D.R.). This
would be admitting that Germany was permanently divided.
The second demand was for the evacuation of Berlin by all
four powers and the handing over of access routes to the
D.D.R. Khrushchev threatened to make a separate peace
treaty with the D.D.R. if these terms were not accepted. The
Western powers refused and as the six months expired, his
bluff was called.

KHRUSHCHEV IN THE U.S.A.

Half-way through the six months time limit, the British Prime
Minister, Harold Macmillan, paid a visit to Moscow, complete with fur hat. It is, however, doubtful if much was
achieved except boosting Macmillan's reputation in Britain.
Much more sensational was the visit of Khrushchev himself to
the United States in September 1959.

Khrushchev and Eisenhower accompanied by their wives in the White House

For years he had been seeking an invitation to the U.S.A., risking insults and refusal. When at last the invitation arrived, Khrushchev knew that in the eyes of the world the Soviet Union was at last fully accepted as the equal of the U.S.A. The meeting of Eisenhower and Khrushchev on the tarmac of Andrews Air Base near Washington brought together the two most powerful men in the world. Naturally, the arrival of the world's leading Communist in the capital of the world's leading capitalist power created a delicate situation. There were misunderstandings on both sides. Khrushchev's boasts of Soviet space achievements embarrassed the Americans, while he himself had to listen to an unpleasant speech from the Mayor of Los Angeles. However, his discussions with Eisenhower at Camp David marked the high point of good relations between the super-powers during the 'cold war'. Mrs Khrushchev impressed many Americans with her warmth and charm. Khrushchev himself flew back to Moscow full of praise for Eisenhower. The Chinese, however, greeted these remarks with outraged horror. To them Khrushchev was a coward who was betraying the revolution.

THE U-2 FLIGHT

After his American visit, Khrushchev pressed on with his long-term ambition—a meeting of the Big Four, Eisenhower, de Gaulle, Macmillan and himself. China's leaders would never sit at the same table as the Americans but nevertheless a summit meeting of the Big Four might prove useful. Eventually it was agreed to meet in Paris in May 1960. The meeting never took place. On 1 May an American U-2 reconnaissance plane was shot down near Sverdlovsk in the Ural Mountains. For several years there unarmed high-speed jets, equipped with telescopic cameras, had been flying high across the Soviet Union photographing strategic regions. At last an anti-aircraft unit equipped with missiles succeeded in bringing one down and the pilot, Captain Francis G. Powers, was captured.

Khrushchev arrived in Paris on 14 May, accompanied by Defence Minister Rodion Malinovsky. He immediately announced that he would not sit at the conference table unless the U-2 flights were cancelled, those responsible punished and

Eisenhower apologised. On the 16th, Eisenhower announced cancellation of U-2 flights but refused to apologise for them. The next day, after a stormy press conference, Khrushchev returned to Moscow. Unwilling to destroy completely the 'spirit of Camp David', he continued to insist that Eisenhower was not responsible for the flights.

It seems that Khrushchev was having second thoughts about the Summit Conference. As we have noted, the Chinese were bitterly opposed to his courtship of the U.S.A. in 1959. Relations with China had been cooling off since 1955 when Khrushchev had patched up the Soviet quarrel with Yugoslavia. The Chinese were angered by his attack on Stalin's memory at the Twentieth Party Congress in 1956. Arguments began to grow about the meaning of Communism and how it should be applied at home and in dealing with foreign states. Remarks of Khrushchev's, such as that the U.S.A. and U.S.S.R. should work together to maintain the peace of the world, were calculated to infuriate the Chinese. This was practically saying that revolutionary Communism should cease.

In wrecking the Summit Conference, Khrushchev was probably trying to show the Communist world that he was quite capable of getting tough with the Western capitalist nations. For the next three years relations between the Soviet Union and the West were generally at a low ebb.

KHRUSHCHEV AT THE UNITED NATIONS

Three months after the collapse of the Summit, Khrushchev set off on his second visit to the U.S.A. accompanied by several East European Communist leaders. This time his destination was the United Nations building in New York, where an impressive gathering of world statesmen assembled. Only de Gaulle was absent, and of course Mao Tse-Tung and Adenauer, whose respective countries are not members of U.N.O.

An attempt to bring Khrushchev and Eisenhower together again failed. The former did little to regain his reputation in the U.N. Assembly where he made personal attacks on the Secretary-General Dag Hammarskjöld and beat his desk with a shoe to show his disapproval of another's speech. He also won publicity by visiting the cheap Harlem Hotel in which the Cuban leader, Fidel Castro, was staying.

Two months later, as Eisenhower's term of office drew to an end, presidential elections were held in the U.S.A. Senator John F. Kennedy won by a narrow margin over Vice-President Richard Nixon and assumed office in January 1961.

The Berlin Wall

'*I am a Berliner*'—President Kennedy in Berlin, 1963

A LUCKY ESCAPE

Hans Puhl was on patrol in the American sector of Berlin. He was twenty-two years of age, German born and a U.S. military policeman. Suddenly he and his companions in their jeep heard shots. When they reached the scene of the shooting, they raced up to the third floor of a nearby block of flats and looked out over the Russian sector. The battle was between West German Police (Schupos) and East German People's Police (Vopos). The prize was a young East German, Michael Meyer, who lay just inside the Eastern sector with five bullets in his arms and chest. As Hans Puhl watched, two Vopos seized Meyer's wrists and began dragging him away. Hans raced downstairs and across the road, pointed his pistol through the barbed wire and ordered the Vopos to release him. With the help of firemen Meyer was rescued and later recovered in hospital. He was one of the many hundreds of East Germans who since August 1961 have risked their lives trying to escape under, through or over the Berlin Wall. Meyer was lucky but he marked his escape by a sticky trail of blood right up the Wall over which the firemen pulled him to safety.

THE DIVIDED CITY

Kennedy and Khrushchev met for the first time in June 1961 in Vienna. The events of the following eighteen months seem to show that the Soviet leader was not impressed by the younger President (Khrushchev was sixty-seven and Kennedy forty-four). The spotlight was again turned on Germany, where the stream of emigrants through West Berlin from the

The construction of the Berlin Wall

D.D.R. was creating difficulties. Industrial production and building programmes in the D.D.R. were falling behind schedule. This was hardly surprising since the D.D.R. had lost well over 3½ million citizens since 1945—about 850 per day.

On 10 August, Walter Ulbricht, Prime Minister of the D.D.R., addressed factory workers: 'The frontiers of our republic will be protected at any cost. We will do everything to stop the criminal activity of the headhunters, the slave traders of Western Germany and the American Spies!' Three days later under the watchful eyes of the Vopos, workmen began building the Wall, completely sealing off the Eastern sector of the city. The feeling of the Western powers was expressed by an American journalist, William Chamberlin, who visited Berlin in 1962.

'This is a fantastic sight, the first time a great city has been slashed in two by a big ugly barrier eight feet high, built of concrete and cinder blocks with strands of barbed wire across the top. At more or less regular intervals are watch towers manned by two policemen armed with pistols and machine-guns, on the look-out for anyone trying to escape what is now brutally, nakedly, visibly the huge penitentiary of the Soviet Zone.'

The building of the Wall broke the terms of the four-power agreement on Berlin. Some Americans advised Kennedy to order his troops in Berlin to tear down the Wall. Kennedy wisely refused since the Russians were far stronger there and might leave America no choice but to use heavier and heavier weapons. However, he sent General Clay, the hero of the 1948-9 airlift, as his personal representative in the city. Nevertheless the Wall remained and claimed forty-one victims during the first fifteen months after it was built. By that time, even Berlin was temporarily forgotten as a much more serious threat was endangering the peace and safety of the world.

The Cuba Crisis

'*One does not commit suicide over trifles*'—Alexander Pushkin, Russian poet

VITAL PHOTOGRAPHS

Early on Sunday morning 14 October 1962 a torrential downpour of rain fell on the Central American island of Cuba. The weather had been stormy for several weeks but later that morning the clouds began to disperse and the sun shone brightly. Ninety miles away at the U.S. Air Base of Key West, Major Rudolf Anderson was preparing to take off in his U-2 reconnaissance plane—his destination Cuba. Anti-aircraft gunners on the island found their electrical controls had been put out of action by the rain, so Anderson was able to make a low-level flight unhindered. He took many photographs which were quickly developed and dispatched to Washington. Defence experts found their worst fears revealed. On 16 October a special report was delivered to President Kennedy informing him that Soviet rocket sites and bomber forces were rapidly being established on the island of Cuba, aimed at the heart of America like a dagger thrust.

COMMUNISM IN THE CARIBBEAN

A few months after the death of Stalin, a young lawyer was brought to trial in Havana, the Cuban capital. Although he had spent two-and-a-half months in solitary confinement he defended himself with skill. Nevertheless, he was found guilty of plotting to overthrow Batista's government and sentenced to fifteen years imprisonment. Released in 1956 he went to Mexico, formed an 'army' and returned to Cuba. After two years of struggle and disappointments, he finally overthrew Batista and became President of Cuba on 1 January 1959. His name was Fidel Castro.

The bearded Fidel Castro with Ben Bella of Algeria

Castro's behaviour soon began to alarm his mighty neighbour to the north. He nationalised American sugar plantations, factories and oil refineries. As a result President Eisenhower broke off relations with Cuba in January 1961, but a few months later Kennedy went even further. Persuaded that Castro was unpopular with the Cuban people, Kennedy allowed a group of exiles to invade the island at the 'Bay of Pigs'. The Cuban exiles were utterly routed, but fearing that American troops would follow, Castro asked the Russians for help.

Since Cuba was the first state of the whole American continent to become Communist, Khrushchev felt compelled to sustain it. So it came about that by the summer of 1962 the Soviet build-up was well under way. This could not be hidden from the Americans, but it was Major Anderson's flight which provided the final proof.

THE BRINK OF WAR

President Kennedy had three possible ways of ridding Cuba of the Soviet missiles and bombers. The first was full-scale invasion of Cuba by U.S. troops. This would not only involve heavy loss of life but would certainly lead to fighting between the invading Americans and the thousands of Russians stationed on the island. The result of this could only be World War III. This would also be the result of the second possibility —an air strike against the Soviet bases. The third possibility, a naval blockade of Cuba, seemed to carry the least risk of war.

On 23 October President Kennedy signed the proclamation authorising the blockade:

'I, John F. Kennedy, President of the United States of America, do hereby proclaim that the forces under my command are ordered, beginning at 2 p.m. 24th October, 1962, to interdict delivery of offensive weapons and associated materials to Cuba. . . .

'Any vessel or craft which may be proceeding towards Cuba may be intercepted and may be directed to identify itself, its cargo, equipment and stores and its port of call, to stop, to lie to, to submit to visit and search or to proceed as directed. . . .'

The following day the Soviet tanker *Bucharest* was intercepted by U.S. warships but allowed to proceed to Havana. Twelve of the twenty-five freighters following were, however, ordered to turn back by the Soviet authorities before interception. Round one had gone to Kennedy, but the problem of the rocket bases on Cuba still remained. On 26 October Kennedy increased the pressure by letting it be known that 'further action' was being considered. Khrushchev must have believed that an invasion of Cuba was being prepared with all its unthinkable consequences. At last he called a halt. The man who had seen the agony of Stalingrad and the devastation of the

Ukraine with his own eyes, could not bring himself to order the suicide of the Soviet Union. At 4 a.m. (Moscow time), on the 27th, a telegram arrived in Washington indicating that rockets would be dismantled in return for a guarantee not to invade Cuba.

WAR AVOIDED

Victory was Kennedy's but he did not seek to humiliate Khrushchev. Instead he praised the Soviet leader's wisdom and statesmanship. Only these two men, the most powerful in the world, realised how close to nuclear war they had come. Both were too sobered and relieved by their escape to try to secure any advantage. On the contrary, the two super-powers finally and fully understood that no political quarrel could be worth pursuing to the point of nuclear war.

The rest of the world stood by helplessly, as the two giants faced each other. America's allies in Europe were informed of her decisions and actions which they generally supported. They could not have altered them whatever they had thought. As the U.S. and Soviet delegates argued in the U.N. General

C.N.D. supporters oppose U.S. action over Cuba

Assembly, the great mass of Afro-Asian states sat helplessly by. China was naturally infuriated by what it considered Khrushchev's surrender. There seems no doubt that his failure in the Cuban crisis helped to bring about his downfall two years later. In the face of overwhelming American strength, Khrushchev wisely backed down just as Kennedy had done over the Berlin Wall.

The Test Ban Treaty

'It seems to me, Mr President, that the time has come to put an end to nuclear tests once and for all', wrote Khrushchev to Kennedy two months after the Cuba crisis. At that time there were only four nuclear powers in the world—the U.S.A., the U.S.S.R., Britain and France. The first French atomic test had taken place less than three years before, so their power was extremely limited. China's first test was still eighteen months away. The future of Britain's nuclear forces was in some doubt, but in any case they were only 5 per cent of America's strength.

Only the U.S.A. and the U.S.S.R. are genuine nuclear powers. They alone have the strength to destroy each other even after being attacked first. Mainly as a result of their experience over Cuba, the American and Soviet governments were able to agree to the terms of a treaty banning the testing of nuclear weapons on or above the earth's surface. The Test Ban Treaty was signed in Moscow in August 1963 by representatives of the U.S.S.R., the U.S.A. and Britain. Dozens of other states added their names to the treaty but neither France nor China did. At the time of writing only these two countries have exploded nuclear weapons above ground since 1963.

Another valuable development was the setting up of a teleprinter communication link between Washington and Moscow via England and Sweden. The link, known as the 'Hot Line', enables instant communication between U.S. and Soviet leaders in an emergency. For example a U.S. rocket might go off course and approach Soviet territory. The 'Hot Line' could warn the Russians of the mistake and perhaps prevent them from firing rockets at the U.S.A.

The End of an Era

The events of 1962–3 seemed to mark a definite change in the way in which the two super-powers regarded and treated each other. Fear of the U.S.S.R. which filled the minds of the Western nations during the 1940s and 1950s has largely disappeared. The French do not believe that there is any need for U.S. troops in Europe now. Fear of the U.S.S.R. has been replaced in some minds by that of China. Since the Berlin crisis of 1961, world politics have swung further and further away from Europe; 1962 saw the Cuban crisis and Chinese attacks on northern India; by 1964 Vietnam was beginning to dominate the headlines. Africa also saw a succession of revolutions and similar troubles.

The men who fashioned the politics of the late 1950s and early 1960s disappeared rapidly from the world scene. Macmillan and Adenauer both retired in October 1963, a few weeks before the assassination of President Kennedy in Dallas,

L to R: President Kennedy, Premier Nehru, Vice-President Johnson

Texas. Jawaharlal Nehru died in May 1964 after leading India through sixteen difficult years. Five months later Khrushchev fell from power. Harold Wilson brought Labour back to power in Britain after thirteen years, and China became the world's fifth nuclear power. Mao Tse Tung, China's leader, remained in office as did Charles de Gaulle until 1969. By this time, a new U.S. President, Richard Nixon, had been elected.

Evidence of the new role of the Soviet Union came in 1966 when Khrushchev's successor Alexei Kosygin brought to an end the Indo-Pakistan War. He persuaded President Ayub Khan and Prime Minister Shastri to join him in Tashkent to sign a Peace Treaty. In her dealings with her own close allies the Soviet Union proved to be as tough as it had always been.

Early in 1968 Alexander Dubček took over the Czechoslovak Communist Party and pledged a number of popular reforms such as the abolition of censorship. Although stressing his loyalty to the Warsaw Pact, Dubček alarmed the Soviet leaders. Probably they thought Dubček's 'liberalism' would spread to the U.S.S.R. Talks were held between Russian and Czech leaders but in August 1968 Russian and other East European troops invaded Czechoslovakia. Unlike Hungary in 1956 there was little bloodshed but 40,000 Czechs fled their country. By early 1969 Dubček and his reforms had been dropped. That the Russians were still anxious to keep the peace was, however, shown by their signing treaties with West Germany (1970) and in 1972 with the U.S.A. to limit nuclear weapons.

In her dealings with her communist neighbours in East Europe, however, the Soviet Union proved to be as tough in 1968, if not as brutal, as she had been in 1956. Under her Communist Party Secretary, Alexander Dubcek, Czechoslovakia began to introduce sweeping liberal reforms. After repeated meetings and warnings the Russian army accompanied by other Warsaw Pact units invaded Czechoslovakia in August 1968. Although there was little fighting the reformers in Czechoslovakia were steadily driven from office. It was clear that the Soviet leaders were not prepared to allow new ideas to flourish which might threaten their own positions.

5   The End of the European Empires

The Dwarfing of Europe

'The problem of the twentieth century . . . is colour'—William Du Bois, U.S. Negro Leader, 1900

THIRTY YEARS ON

In July 1930 a young Indian politician was sent to gaol for the 'crime' of campaigning to make his country free of British rule. 'I had gone back to gaol after nearly seven years', he wrote, 'and memories of prison life had somewhat faded. I was in Naini Central Prison . . . my enclosure was . . . circular in shape with a diameter of about 100 feet and with a circular wall about fifteen feet high surrounding it. In the middle was a drab and ugly building containing four cells. I was given two of these. After the exciting and very active life I had been leading outside, I felt rather lonely and depressed.'[1]

Thirty years later, the ex-inmate of Naini Prison gave a dinner party in Delhi. There were 125 guests, including the Vice-President of India and several princes. The principal guests were Her Majesty Queen Elizabeth II and the Duke of Edinburgh who were making a royal tour of southern Asia. The ex-prisoner's name was Jawaharlal Nehru, and in 1961 he was completing thirteen years as Prime Minister of the Republic of India. He remained Prime Minister until his death in May 1964.

THE COLONIAL REVOLT

These two episodes from Nehru's life illustrate the most important political change in the world since 1945—the end of

[1] J. Nehru, *Autobiography*, Bodley Head, new edn., 1942.

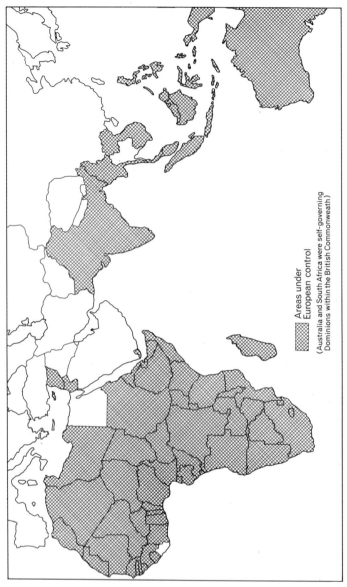

Afro-Asian Colonial Empires: 1939

Areas under
European control

(Australia and South Africa were self-governing
Dominions within the British Commonweath)

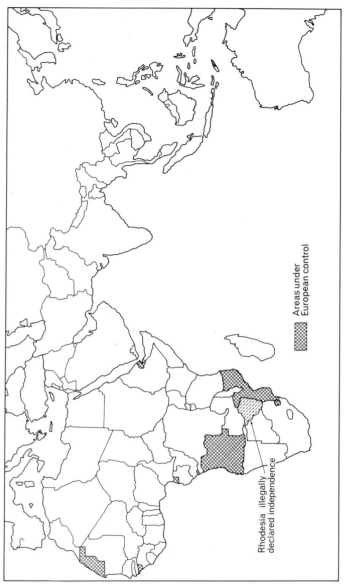

Rhodesia illegally
declared independence

Areas under
European control

Afro-Asian Colonial Empires: 1968

Europe's great colonial empires in Asia and Africa. In 1939, as you can see on the map on p. 106, these empires were vast and on the surface seemed secure. People who protested against European rule as Nehru did served many gaol sentences. Now scarcely a quarter of a century since World War II, these empires have almost completely disappeared. In 1945 there were fifty-one founder members of U.N.O. By 1967 the number had risen to almost 120. Most, but not all, of the newcomers were ex-colonies with a total population of about 1,000 million people. This revolt of colonial peoples against the West was mainly completed in the twenty years after 1945, but it did not develop suddenly or without warning. Its roots can be traced back to the nineteenth century.

WHY THE REVOLUTION CAME

Europeans began settling in overseas territory late in the fifteenth century, and continued in varying degrees until 1914. The largest annexations took place in the nineteenth century, especially the carve-up of Africa after 1880. It is not necessary here to discuss why Europeans sought colonies except to say that the principal reasons were to make money out of them, to provide new homelands for settlers or to use them as military bases.

Long before 1914 overseas territories had begun throwing off European rule or successfully resisting European efforts to take over. The Americans led the way, declaring independence from Britain in 1776. This and the Revolution of 1789 inspired the peoples of Latin America under Spanish and Portuguese rule. By 1830 all Central and South America was free apart from a few small territories and the islands of the West Indies. Later in the nineteenth century the French attempt to take over Mexico and the Italian attempt in Abyssinia were complete failures. In spite of these failures, the modern arms of Europeans, especially the machine-gun, enabled them to crush any native opposition with ease.

The tide turned in 1904–5. The mighty Russian Empire clashed with the 'tiny' Japanese Empire over control of Far Eastern territories. In a few months the Russian armies were routed and her Pacific and Baltic fleets largely disappeared under the waters of the Yellow Sea and the Korean Strait.

The myth of European invincibility was broken. Following the defeat of his army and navy the Russian Czar faced a revolution at home. Although crushed, the revolution created shock waves which spread across Asia—to Turkey, India, Persia, China and even Vietnam. By 1914 revolutionary ideas were circulating in the Middle East and Asia.

World War I helped the cause of independence. The spectacle of Europeans fighting a vast civil war lost them the respect of their colonial subjects. Indeed Germans, British and French encouraged the colonies of their enemies to revolt, especially in the Middle East. Speeches by President Wilson and Lenin attacked imperialism (empire-building). These were warmly received by Asian revolutionaries such as Nehru, Ho Chi Minh (Indo-China) and Tan Malaka (Dutch East Indies).

Meanwhile, the old 'white' colonies of the British Empire were moving quickly towards complete self-government. At the Versailles Peace Conference in 1919, Canada, South Africa, Australia and New Zealand were represented separately. Even India was allowed its own representative. Two years later Ireland secured its independence from Britain after a five-year struggle, providing another example to colonial peoples. If white peoples could receive independence there could be no valid reason for refusing to grant it to 'coloured' peoples except on the grounds of racialism.

India set the pace amongst the 'coloured' nations. As early as 1885 a Congress Party had been set up to promote the cause of self-government. By 1919 Britain was forced to yield ground. Indians were allowed to take a limited share in national government and a greater share in local affairs. The Congress Party was not satisfied with this, nor with the British Government's handover of more power in 1935.

Following the Indian example a Pan-African Congress met for the first time in 1919. It had little effect but was a clear indication of things to come. Thus by 1939 it would be true to say that revolutionary movements were active in all parts of Asia and Africa. Many Europeans were aware of this but refused to withdraw for fear of an enemy moving in behind.

WORLD WAR II AND THE COLONIES

Having paved the way in 1904–5, Japan completed the destruction of the white man's image between 1940 and 1943. In those years she overran much of the Pacific and south-east Asia and reached the eastern gates of India. Puppet governments were set up in the place of the colonial governors and officials. Resistance movements led by Communists and nationalists fought against the Japanese invaders. When the Japanese were eventually driven out the resistance groups had no intention of calmly handing back power to their former white masters. They wanted independence and were prepared to fight for it if necessary. Although never conquered by the Axis powers the nations of the Middle East realised their importance through the possession of oil. They were able to press for early independence. So also were the colonies in Africa south of the Sahara. In return for their support General de Gaulle had to promise that colonial subjects would become equal citizens of France with the right to send deputies to Paris.

The colonial revolt was spearheaded by educated groups of men throughout the European empires. By the 1940s large numbers of colonial subjects had returned to their homelands after extensive education in the West. Nehru and the Malaysian Prime Minister, Tengku Abdul Rahman, went to Cambridge; Kwame Nkrumah, President of Ghana (1957–66), went to Lincoln University in the U.S.A. For those not able to travel, the development of the cinema and radio brought the sights and sounds of the outside world to remote villages. The pre-1914 days of ignorance, illiteracy and superstition were rapidly passing away for large numbers of colonial subjects.

AFTER 1945

For several weeks after the retreat of the Japanese, the resistance forces were free from interference in Indo-China and Indonesia. Neither the French nor the Dutch were able to return and had to rely upon the British and American forces to re-establish government in the colonies. This breathing space gave the revolutionaries time to declare their independence and prepare for the coming fight. In Britain the election of a Labour Government indicated early independence for India. The urge to build and keep empires was also dying in Europe. The British Chancellor of the Exchequer, Hugh Dalton, said, 'I don't believe one person in a hundred thousand in this

Presidents Nkrumah and Nasser

country cares tuppence about India so long as British people
are not being mauled about there'. With a few exceptions such
as the Belgian Congo, overseas possessions had cost far more
than they earned. As events were to prove, economic disaster
did not follow the granting of independence.

If Europeans no longer cared for colonialism, the two super-
powers made no secret of their complete opposition to it. This
obviously encouraged revolutionaries throughout the colonial
world and weakened the morale of their European masters.

Finally, of course, example played a large part in the spread
of the colonial revolution. With the development of modern
telecommunications and rapid air travel it was not possible to
conceal the successes of newly won independence from colonial
subjects. The colonial revolution began in Asia and the Middle
East in the second half of the 1940s, spread to North Africa in
the early fifties and moved on to West, Central and East Africa
in the late fifties and early sixties.

Violent Revolutions in Asia, 1945–57

'Political power grows out of the barrel of a gun'—Mao Tse-Tung, 1938

At the foot of the mountains where the frontiers of China, Burma, Vietnam and Thailand almost meet, there lies a great plain eleven miles long and three miles wide. It is shaped like an oak leaf and surrounded by jagged peaks rising to 2,000 feet. At 10.40 on the morning of 20 November 1953, sixty Dakota aircraft flew over the plain and out of them dropped 3,000 French paratroopers. One crashed to his death as his parachute failed to open, two died of bullet wounds before landing and eleven others were injured on landing. Four hours later another battalion was dropped and for the time being the enemy melted away. Operation 'Castor' was under way.

The inhabitants of one of the villages crouched in their wood and straw huts, as the heavily armed sky-soldiers searched for enemy stragglers, dug trenches and gabbled into radio transmitters. Although they did not know it, the name of their village was to echo round the world six months later. For the French landed on that plain to tempt the revolutionary army —the Viet Minh—into the open battle. Supplied by 80,000 porters each pushing a 4-cwt load on a bicycle, the Viet Minh accepted the challenge. They dragged field guns onto the peaks above the plain and began pounding the French strongpoint below. Attacking recklessly in 'human waves', they forced the French back to an ever smaller area. On the morning of 6 May 1954 the final attack was mounted and 10,000 French and colonial troops were marched off into captivity. The village is called Dien Bien Phu.

INDO-CHINA

The French Empire of Indo-China was composed of three separate states—Laos, Cambodia and Vietnam. In Vietnam an independence movement called the Viet Minh was set up in 1941. The leaders were Ho Chi Minh and Vo Nguyen Giap, both veteran Communists. On 2 September 1945 they declared Vietnam independent. Ho was elected President. Early in 1946 the French were persuaded to recognise a free Vietnam

and Ho went to Paris to sign the agreement. Later in the year
the French turned on the Viet Minh and so began a bitter war
which lasted until the fall of Dien Bien Phu. Before it finished,
the French had lost 75,000 dead and spent £3,000 million
fighting the war.

At first, the French underestimated the Viet Minh who
were repeatedly able to retreat across the Chinese frontier
when hard-pressed. In October 1950 Nguyen Giap's army
overran a series of French forts in the north and advanced on

Attacking the Viet Minh with mortars

Hanoi. The new French commander, Marshal de Lattre de
Tassigny, broke the Viet Minh attack, which cost them 6,000
dead. After this they returned to guerrilla warfare, taking control of the countryside and smaller towns. It was in an effort to
repeat the success of de Lattre de Tassigny that his successor
General Navarre ordered the establishment of the camp at
Dien Bien Phu. It was an important route junction but it was
the worst possible spot to choose. It could be supplied only by
air, it was dominated by the surrounding hills, and it became a
sea of mud during the rains. 'We have them now', said General
Giap when he learnt that the French were staying. Two months

later, in July 1954 at the Geneva Conference, the French agreed to leave Vietnam, which was partitioned. The North became Communist whilst the South was supposed to become a democracy.

INDONESIA

As mentioned in Chapter 3, the Republic of Indonesia was declared by the subjects of the Dutch East Indies only two days after Japan's surrender. With no troops in Asia the Dutch had to rely on British troops to move in and take control of their former empire. When the Dutch returned and tried to take over, fighting broke out with the Indonesian revolutionaries, The task was hopeless from the start. Three thousand islands and eighty million people could not be subdued by a small European state which had just undergone five years of Nazi occupation. By early 1947 Indonesia had gained so much support abroad and the Dutch had become so weary that a conference was called and independence terms were agreed. Fighting continued for a further two years between Dutch die-hards and the Indonesians on one side and between Indonesian nationalists and Communists on the other. However, in 1950 President Sukarno was able to lead a united Indonesian Republic into the United Nations. The last bit of Dutch territory in the area, West Irian, was handed over to Indonesia in 1963.

MALAYSIA

When British troops returned to the Malay Peninsula they were met by Chin Peng's Communist guerrilla army. Like his counterpart Ho Chi Minh, Chin Peng was determined to take over the reins of government as soon as possible. The British put the nine states under martial law for six months and then formed them into the Malayan Union. They were given some freedom but remained essentially under British control. Singapore was not included in the Union so it was here amongst the large Chinese population that Chin Peng concentrated his effort organising strikes and riots. When in 1948 the Union was transformed into the Federation of Malaya gaining even more self-government, Chin Peng decided to take sterner measures. He ordered his 6,000-strong Malayan

British forces return to Singapore, 1945

Races Liberation Army to begin a reign of terror throughout Malaya. Wealthy Chinese, British and Malayan planters and businessmen were killed or held to ransom. Plantations, villages and trains were attacked. Over 50,000 British troops were drafted to Malaya, about one-sixth as many as the French had in Vietnam. The revolutionaries were beaten in Malaya because the British won over the bulk of the local population. Instead of resisting nationalism as the French did in Vietnam, Britain went along with it.

Malaya received its independence in 1957 and Singapore as a separate state two years later. In 1963 Malaya, Singapore, Sarawak, Brunei and Sabah joined to form the Federation of Malaysia which met with hostility from Indonesia, but fortunately a full-scale war was avoided.

Peaceful Handovers in Asia, 1946–8

' I did not become His Majesty's First Minister in order to preside over the liquidation of the British Empire'—W. S. Churchill in 1940

PHILIPPINES

The first territory to receive independence after World War II was ruled not by Europeans but by the U.S.A. The Philippines had been part of the Spanish Empire until 1899, when they were seized by the Americans. Between 1941 and 1944 they were occupied by the Japanese. When the Americans returned they took over the government temporarily until arrangements for independence were worked out. The 7,000 islands of the Philippines became an independent republic on 4 July 1946.

INDIA AND PAKISTAN

Indian demands for independence had grown steadily throughout the twentieth century. In 1909, 1919 and 1935 parliament had passed Acts each giving successively more power to Indians in the field of self-government. In 1942 the Indian Congress made it quite clear that nothing short of complete independence would prevent growing unrest developing into full-scale rebellion.

One major problem had to be solved before the Labour Government could fulfil its 1945 promise of early independence. There were two great religious groups in India—the Hindus numbering about 330 million, and the Muslims numbering seventy million. During the period of British rule these two groups had tended to grow apart. The Muslims refused to co-operate with the foreigners, therefore the Hindus gained most of the power and privileges available for the native inhabitants. The Muslims feared that independence would mean their suppression. In 1945 the Muslim leader Ali Jinnah declared, 'Only over the dead bodies of Muslims will the Congress Party [Hindu] flag fly in the northern provinces'. He demanded that India should be partitioned—a Muslim state in the north and a Hindu state for the remainder. The Hindus were strongly opposed to this. Clement Attlee broke the deadlock by stating that come what may the British would leave India by June 1948. He sent Admiral Lord Louis Mountbatten to India as Viceroy to prepare for independence.

Mountbatten realised that partition was the only answer. With the co-operation of Indians and British alike, he was able to bring forward the date of independence to 15 August 1947. India remained the Hindu state while the Muslims founded the new state of Pakistan in the north. The Muslim

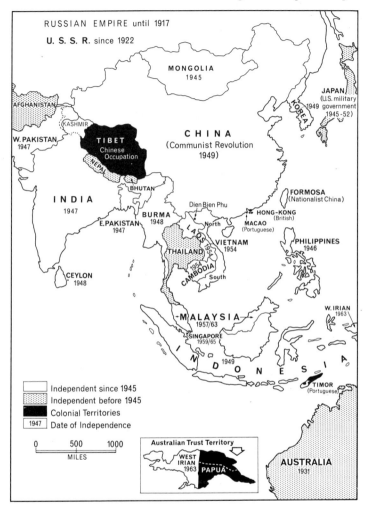

Asian Independence to 1968

population is concentrated in two regions, so Pakistan is a divided state: West and East Pakistan are 1,000 miles apart.

As independence approached, the whole subcontinent became the scene of violence, bloodshed and destruction as Muslims and Hindus tore at each other's throats. The roads were thronged with millions of refugees.[1] Probably half a million people died. Trouble also arose over the northern province of Kashmir which both states claimed. This led to war in 1948–9 and 1965.

Calcutta, 1946

CEYLON

In February 1948 the eight million people of the island of Ceylon chose to remain in the British Commonwealth. Burma, the other great British possession in south Asia, preferred to follow a solitary path.

[1] The violence in India was not directed at or by Europeans therefore the handover was 'peaceful'.

BURMA

Even before the defeat of Japan, a plan for Burmese self-government within the Commonwealth had been drawn up by the British Government. Britain had large financial and business interests in the country which she was keen to restore. The Burmese resistance army, like those in Vietnam and Malaya, wanted immediate independence. Quick action by Attlee prevented revolutionary war. The Union Jack was hauled down on 4 January 1948 and Burma became an independent neutral state.

Independence in the Middle and Near East, 1944–62

The collapse of the Turkish Empire in 1918 raised hopes of independence amongst the Arab nations. By 1939 some success had been achieved. The oilfields of the Middle East made the Arab states conscious of their own importance in the world. In 1945 Egypt, Syria, Iraq, the Lebanon, Transjordan and Saudi Arabia came together to form the Arab League. Their aims were to expel the Europeans—Britain and France—from the Middle and Near East and promote the cause of Arab unity.

Syria and the Lebanon had been granted independence by France in 1944 and the British handed over power in Jordan in 1946. There were two other areas where the colonial powers were strongly entrenched: the British along the Suez Canal and the French in Tunisia, Algeria and Morocco. The Arab states also saw another enemy in their midst—the Jews. In 1917 Balfour, the British Foreign Secretary, had promised the Jews a national homeland in Palestine. Little more than 100,000 moved there in the 1920s, but with the arrival of Hitler on the European scene immigration increased to 35,000 in 1938 alone. After the Nazi horrors there were thousands of Jewish survivors in 1945 who wanted to go to Palestine. To avoid stirring up the Arabs, Britain tried to limit the immigration and was strongly condemned by the Americans and French. Terrorism raged through Palestine. Eventually in May 1948 the new state of Israel came into being and found itself at war with neighbouring Arab states. Israel emerged victorious and Arab nationalism suffered a setback.

EGYPT

The first step in the destruction of Britain's position came with the army rebellion against the corrupt King Farouk in 1952. Colonel Gamal Abdel Nasser emerged as the strongest of the group and became President of Egypt. Nasser agreed that British troops should evacuate Egypt by the end of 1955. At this time Nasser began large-scale trading with the Russians. As a result the Americans withdrew their offer of a large loan towards the cost of the Aswan Dam, a project of vital importance to Egypt's economy.

Nasser's reply was to nationalise the Suez Canal in July 1956, much to the annoyance of Britain and France who owned most of the shares in the Canal Company. The British Prime Minister, Anthony Eden, saw Nasser as an 'Arab Hitler'. In his memoirs Eden wrote, 'A man with Colonel Nasser's record could not be allowed to have his thumb on our windpipe'. The Suez Canal was Britain's vital link with the oilfields and the Far East. What Eden failed to realise was that if Nasser had squeezed Britain's 'windpipe' he might have strangled himself as well, since the majority of ships passing through the Canal for a £5,000 fee each were British.

Eden was determined to win back the Canal. In October

Port Said after the Anglo-French attack

1956 Israel, probably encouraged by Britain and France, attacked Egypt. British and French troops then invaded Egypt to 'protect' the Canal, which the Egyptians promptly blocked with scuttled ships. The invasion of Egypt was the most disastrous decision of the British Government since the Munich Conference in 1938. The whole of the Labour and Liberal parties denounced the Government. Two Conservative Ministers resigned. The Americans were unable to support their allies and naturally the whole Afro-Asian bloc at the U.N. saw it as an imperialist war. To the Russians, busily crushing the Hungarian revolution, it was a heaven-sent opportunity to divert attention away from themselves. Bulganin threatened to attack London and Paris with rockets.

Crushed by a barrage of hostile opinion the British and French halted, and within six weeks had withdrawn all their forces. U.N. troops moved in to supervise the cease-fire and clearing of the Suez Canal. In January 1957, unhappy and ill, Anthony Eden resigned the premiership and was succeeded by Harold Macmillan.

CYPRUS

The Mediterranean island of Cyprus, a British possession since 1878, became another thorny problem in the late 1950s. The majority of the inhabitants of Greek origin wanted union with Greece. The British having lost their Suez base wanted to keep the island and were supported by the Turkish Cypriots. A great deal of blood was spilt before a settlement was reached. Cyprus became a Republic in 1960 with a Greek Cypriot President and a Turkish Cypriot Vice-President, while Britain was allowed to keep her bases.

MOROCCO AND TUNISIA

Meanwhile France had successfully handed over power in two of her North African possessions in March 1956. The French Prime Minister, M. Mendès-France, arranged the settlement in July 1954, a week after the Geneva Conference on Indo-China. Unfortunately, the solution for the third territory, Algeria, was far from quick. Revolution in Algeria broke out in November 1954 and dragged on for over seven weary, bloodstained years.

ALGERIA

There were three obstacles to giving independence to Algeria. First, there were one million European settlers out of a population of nine million who wanted France to keep control. Secondly, Algeria had been a department of France since 1947, sending deputies to Paris. Thirdly, large supplies of oil and natural gas were found in the Sahara in 1956, making Algeria a valuable asset.

In 1952 Ahmed Ben Bella set up an Algerian Revolutionary Committee in Cairo with the aim of securing independence for his country. In 1954, bearing the name National Liberation Front (F.L.N.), the revolution began. For the French having just ended the long bitter war in Indo-China, Algeria was to prove another disaster. Eventually 500,000 troops were

Trouble in Algiers

engaged in trying to hold the territory, at the annual cost of
£750 million. As with most civil wars fighting became steadily
more brutal, both sides using torture and murder.
The problem of Algeria prevented the establishment of a
stable government in France. There were too many conflicting
interests. The army, both in Algeria and in France itself,
presented the greatest threat to liberal democracy. After the
humiliations of 1940, of Dien Bien Phu, and of Suez, the
generals were determined to 'hold' Algeria at all costs.
The first crisis came on 13 May 1958. European mobs ran-
sacked government offices in Algiers and the paratroop
generals seized the opportunity to declare martial law and
take over the reins of the government. For a time it seemed that
the revolution might spread to Paris itself. All parties turned
to the one man whom they thought could solve the problems of
France—Charles de Gaulle. The rebels believed that he would
keep Algeria for France. The Socialists agreed to give him six
months, while even the Communists saw the need for a
'strong man'. On 29 May, President Coty called upon de
Gaulle to form a government of National Safety.
De Gaulle wanted to end the war quickly, but independence
for Algeria could lead to another rebellion amongst the
generals. This happened twice: in January 1960 and more
seriously in April 1961. Speaking over the radio de Gaulle
called upon the army to remain loyal: 'In the name of France
I order that every means be used—and I repeat *every* means to
stop these men. . . . I forbid every Frenchman and, above all,
every soldier, to carry out any of their orders.' The army
rallied to de Gaulle, as did the navy and air force. The four
generals who were leading the revolt were eventually captured and received heavy prison sentences.
Meanwhile, meetings between the French Government and
the F.L.N. were being held at Evian in South-east France.
After early failures, it was eventually agreed in March 1962
that a fully independent Algerian Republic would be
established.
Now came the final bloody chapter of French Algeria.
'Die-hard' Europeans of the Secret Army Organisation
(O.A.S.) made a last desperate attempt to hold Algeria.
Bombs were hurled into cafés, shops and houses, even at

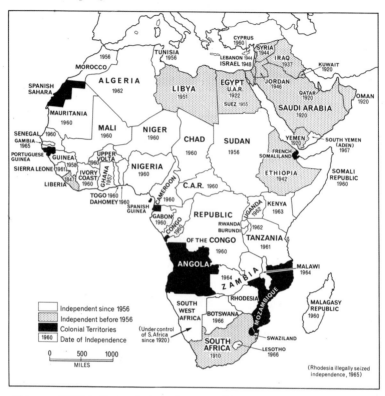

African and Middle Eastern Independence to 1968

queues of Europeans waiting for tickets to France. Arab
children were run down by European cars. When French
soldiers were killed, a week-long battle raged through the
European suburb of Bab el Oued. As the flight of Europeans
continued the O.A.S. realised that they had lost and decided
to destroy everything of value. The library of Algiers University
and some forty schools were burnt down in June 1962.
Refrigerators, washing machines and even cars were hurled
off cliff-tops into the sea. Attempts were made to kill de
Gaulle. All was in vain.

On 3 July 1962, at the cost of a quarter of a million lives,
Algeria became independent.

Independence in Africa, 1951–66

'*There is a wind of change blowing through Africa*'—Harold Macmillan, 1960

The first African territory to gain its freedom was the kingdom of Ethiopia in 1942, although admittedly it had been an Italian colony for less than six years. Another Italian ex-colony, Libya, received its independence in 1951, while further south, in the same year, Kwame Nkrumah became Prime Minister of the Gold Coast. In March 1957 the Gold Coast received complete independence, taking the name of Ghana, thus becoming the first completely *new* African state.

There is no doubt that African territories south of the Sahara were encouraged by the success of the Arab states. The failure of Britain and France at Suez in 1956 showed that Africans could successfully defy Europeans. A few months later Ghanaian independence set an example for the rest of Africa. Britain realised that independence must eventually come to all her territories but only after long and careful preparation. France sought to make her African subjects into Frenchmen. Belgium did not expect to surrender control for thirty years. Portugal had no intention (and still has none) of surrendering control, because she claimed that the territories are part of Portugal itself. The tide of African nationalism was so strong that the British, French and Belgians quickly gave way and handed over power rapidly. Only Portugal has resisted.

THE FRENCH COMMUNITY

The presence of a million Europeans was the main reason why France sought to keep Algeria. South of Algeria were the two enormous French territories of West and Equatorial Africa. Only 80,000 of the twenty million inhabitants were Europeans while the territories themselves were comparatively poor. These territories had been loyal during World War II so there had been no need to fight for them, but nationalism was strong so de Gaulle suggested that the territories should form a community of self-governing states. Of the twelve states involved only Guinea chose to cut herself off completely from France in September 1958. De Gaulle replied by cutting off all aid to

Guinea. The community lasted barely two years. By August 1960 all the members chose complete independence though still maintaining strong links with France.

THE CONGO

The movement towards freedom in the French parts of Africa during the late 1950s spread across the Congo River to Belgium's solitary African colony. Covering over 900,000 square miles of dense tropical forest, more than four times the size of France, the Congo is particularly rich in minerals and rubber. Belgium neither wanted to hand over power nor had she made any preparations to do so.

Political activity developed so rapidly in 1958 and 1959 that the Belgians panicked. A conference called in Brussels in January 1960 announced that power would be handed over on 30 June that year. This allowed only six months to prepare for independence a people who had never known a parliament or general election, who possessed 300 dialects and no common language and amongst whom there was not one senior civil servant, police officer or qualified doctor!

Independence was followed by a mass flight of Belgians from the country leaving hospitals without doctors, schools without teachers and government offices without staff. A fierce quarrel broke out between the two leading politicians, Joseph Kasavubu and Patrice Lumumba. All hope of stable government disappeared when the Security Forces mutinied and ran wild. Belgian paratroops were dispatched to restore order and

Patrice Lumumba

were succeeded by U.N. troops who remained in the Congo
from September 1960 to July 1964.

BRITISH AFRICA

The year 1960 marked the end of the Belgian and French
Empires in Africa and also saw the speeding up of decolonisa-
tion by Britain with the independence of Nigeria. The following year Tanganyika became free. Britain was faced with two
possible 'Algerias' in Kenya and Southern Rhodesia. Both
had large European settler populations, though nothing on
the scale of Algeria itself. In Kenya the central issue was over
the rich 'White Highlands' farmed by Europeans. One
rebellion by a secret society called the Mau Mau took four

A Mau-mau suspect

years to put down (1952-6). Some 10,000 deaths were re-
corded in an area inhabited by one million people. Nevertheless, the demand for independence rose again in the early
1960s and could not be stilled. In December 1963 Kenya
gained independence, fortunately with goodwill on both sides.

At the time of writing the Rhodesian problem remains un-
solved. Rhodesia had a large measure of self-government (by
Europeans) since 1922. In 1953 it joined Northern Rhodesia
and Nyasaland in a Federation, but this broke up when the

latter two became independent in 1964, known as Zambia and Malawi respectively. No satisfactory arrangement could be made for Rhodesia's independence since the Europeans want to remain in control. In November 1965 Rhodesia declared illegal independence, but her claim was not recognised by anyone, and late in 1966 United Nations action was directed against the 'Smith' régime.

PORTUGUESE AFRICA

By the early 1970s only Portugal had withstood the 'wind of change' in Africa. Events in the Congo led to a nationalist rebellion in neighbouring Angola in 1961. The Portuguese dictator, Dr Antonio Salazar, sent thousands of troops to Angola and crushed the rebellion with considerable severity.

The Portuguese territories of Angola and Mozambique, with Rhodesia and South Africa, form a solid block of European power in the south of the continent. Only the weak and newly independent states of Botswana (1966), Lesotho (1966) and Swaziland (1968) lie within this block. To the north, European rule has almost completely disappeared, apart from a few footholds. The largest of these is the desert territory of Spanish Sahara inhabited by about a million Arab tribesmen.

Europe and the New Nations

'Great Britain has lost an Empire but has not yet found a role'— Dean Acheson, 1961

The loss of these empires was a sign of Europe's reduced position in the world. Faced with the opposition of the U.S.A., the U.S.S.R., China and most of the United Nations, European powers could no longer act as they had been doing in the 1930s and earlier. As Algeria and Cyprus had shown, it was impossible to hold a territory in the face of determined and widespread opposition.

Having lost power overseas, Europeans have sought to replace it with influence. Britain has tried hard to develop a multiracial Commonwealth, which has so far survived because it is neither a military, political nor economic alliance.

The Queen receives Commonwealth Prime Ministers, 1966

It is thus able to absorb stresses and strains such as the resignation of South Africa and the Rhodesian question because it has no exact definition. One writer in *The Times* in 1964 called the Commonwealth 'a gigantic farce'. However, because it embraces almost every colour, religion and political belief, it is a 'world in miniature' and could be a valuable force in a troubled world.

France too has very strong links with her ex-African colonies, including Algeria. The memory of the war in Indo-China tended to make the French ignore Asia for a very long time. But in 1966 President de Gaulle received a tremendous reception in Cambodia and also began criticising the American action in Vietnam. Perhaps the greatest adjustment which Europeans have had to make is over the colour question. For generations Africans and Asians were looked upon as inferiors or as children in need of guidance. Having become independent states with equal voting rights in the United Nations

General Assembly, the Afro-Asian nations expect equal treatment. Older Europeans who remember the colonial days sometimes find this change in status hard to accept.

AID PROGRAMMES

The end of colonialism did not mean that the new nations were economically independent. It was quickly realised that they would need financial and technical help for a long time to come.

The French have been the most generous; in 1960 they gave £251 million in aid to Africa: more than the U.S.A., the U.S.S.R. and Britain combined. And in 1963 they combined with their partners in the 'Six' to sign an Association Convention with eighteen newly independent African states. This provided for some 367 projects costing £260 million during the period 1964–9. These projects cover a variety of improvements such as the building of roads, railways, bridges, schools, agricultural stations, hospitals and wells.

In order to increase trade between the 'Six' and the 'eighteen', duties on imports are being steadily reduced. To help the African economies special reductions in duties on tropical products such as cocoa and fruits have been made. Funds have also been made available to stabilise prices.

Though the 'Six' are now showing the way in aid schemes, the original example came from Britain. Parliament passed Acts in 1929, 1940 and 1945 to provide help for the welfare and economies of the Colonies. In 1948 the Colonial Development Corporation was set up to help industrial and agricultural expansion in the Colonies. Britain also played a leading role in the Colombo Plan, started in 1950 to build up the economies of the emerging territories in southern Asia.

Most wealthy countries now look upon aid programmes as a solemn duty. Even a small country like Switzerland has been able to play its part by sending hydroelectric engineers to Nepal. President Kennedy founded the Peace Corps in America through which well-qualified young men and women are persuaded to spend a year in an underdeveloped country. Britain has set up a similar body in the V.S.O. (Voluntary Service Overseas), and the idea is taking root elsewhere. Both the super-powers have been very generous in their aid, as have wealthy countries outside Europe such as Australia, Canada and more recently Japan.

In the 1970s there is still a wide gap between the rich industrialised countries around the N. Atlantic and the W. Pacific and the poorer agricultural countries of Asia, Africa and Latin America. It is most unlikely that the global resources of energy and raw material are sufficient for all the world to enjoy the same living standards as, say, Denmark.

Meanwhile the 'newly' independent nations still face immense problems compared with which those of the 'West' seem very slight. Political struggles use up scarce energy and resources, often with ugly results. Even more difficult are those problems concerned with fast-growing populations and the need to increase food supplies in the face of natural disasters. Two areas of the world, West Africa and the Indian subcontinent, suffered these difficulties particularly harshly around 1970.

From 1967–70 Nigeria was torn by civil war when the Eastern Region declared itself independent under the name Biafra. Eventually Biafra was defeated and in the process many thousands of its people starved. An even greater threat to all West Africa has been a long drought throughout the 1960s and early 1970s which threatens to turn much of the region into desert. The hostility between India and Pakistan flared up again in 1971 when East Pakistan declared itself independent from the West under the name of Bangladesh. The Pakistan army regained control on 25 March but by December India became involved and occupied Bangladesh which then secured its independence. In the long term a rapidly increasing population, monsoon and flood damage and recurring droughts offer a bigger threat to the Sub-continent than do the political squabbles.

6 Towards a United Europe

The Relaunching of Europe

THE MESSINA MEETING

The collapse of a scheme for a European Defence Community (see p. 71) came as a bitter blow to 'European minded' statesmen. Jean Monnet, President of the High Authority of the European Coal and Steel Community (E.C.S.C.), expressed his feelings by resigning from his post. He gave his reason that he wished to work for the establishment of a United States of Europe. As there was some difficulty in finding a successor, M. Monnet stayed on as President of E.C.S.C. until 1956. However, he was in close touch with leaders of the Benelux working out plans for promoting European unity. Suggestions had already been made that E.C.S.C. should be widened to take in other forms of power: gas, electricity and the latest source—atomic energy. From the Dutch came a much more sweeping proposal. This was for a complete customs union, ending all restrictions on trade between E.C.S.C. members.

The Common Assembly of E.C.S.C. called upon the Foreign Ministers of the 'Six' (France, West Germany, Italy, Belgium, Netherlands and Luxembourg) to meet and discuss ways of creating closer European unity. This meeting was held at Messina in Sicily on 1 and 2 June 1955. Here the Foreign Ministers issued a statement containing outline plans for a common policy on transport, energy production, economic development and social welfare. They also included the Dutch proposals for a customs union or Common Market and urged that Britain be invited to join. Even more important the Ministers laid down how their targets were to be achieved and the final date by which each stage had to be completed. For the task of preparing detailed reports a committee was set up under the Belgian Foreign Minister, Paul-Henri Spaak.

Prime Minister Macmillan greets M. Paul-Henri Spaak

THE SPAAK REPORT

Spaak and his team of experts worked hard on the plans for
nearly a year. They concentrated first on plans for the creation
of a European Atomic Energy Commission (Euratom) and
then of a European Economic Community or Common
Market for manufactured goods, raw materials and foodstuffs.
M. Spaak realised that the Common Market would be much
the more important of the two, but news of Euratom was of
much greater interest at the time. In particular, it was urgently
discussed as to who should own the fissile material which
could be used to make atomic bombs. M. Monnet, the main
sponsor of Euratom, made it clear that control of the fissile
material would be supranational. Euratom was to be concerned only with the peaceful uses of atomic energy.

The establishment of a Common Market was aimed at
creating 'a large area with a common economic policy, consti-
tuting a powerful production unit and permitting continuous

expansion, increased stability, and accelerated rise of living standards and the development of harmonious relations among the states joined together'.

Briefly, this meant that the six countries with a population of 170 million would eventually form a single economic unit similar to the U.S.A., with no restrictions on movement of goods, raw materials, agricultural produce, money or labour. This large Common Market would lead (according to the Spaak Report) to a rapid expansion of industry providing more advanced products, more work and higher wages.

It was planned that by 1970 all tariffs and restrictions on trade amongst the six would disappear (later this was brought forward to the middle of 1968). Duties on goods coming into the six would pay the same tariff no matter into which country they entered.

THE TREATY OF ROME

The Spaak Report was accepted as the basis of formal treaties creating the European Economic Community (E.E.C.) and Euratom. The two treaties were signed at Rome on 25 March 1957.

There are 248 articles in the Treaty of Rome founding the E.E.C. The following are the most important:

1. Abolition of all tariffs and restrictions on trade amongst the six member states.
2. A common tariff and trade policy towards other countries.
3. Free movement of people, capital and services amongst member states.
4. A common agricultural policy.
5. A common transport policy.
6. Fair and free competition within the E.E.C. (This means that governments and organisations must treat all firms, etc., throughout E.E.C. fairly and without favour, e.g. no subsidies or tax rebates.)

BRITAIN AND EEC—I

You will remember from Chapter 3 that Britain was opposed to supranationalism—that is surrendering control of some part of the nation's life to an outside body. In 1950 Britain had

The European Community

INSTITUTIONS

ECSC	COMMON MARKET	EURATOM
EUROPEAN COAL AND STEEL COMMUNITY	EUROPEAN ECONOMIC COMMUNITY	EUROPEAN ATOMIC ENERGY COMMISION
HIGH AUTHORITY	COMMISSION	COMMISSION
	RUN THE COMMUNITY AND MAKE POLICIES	

ONE COUNCIL OF MINISTERS

MAKE FINAL DECISIONS ON POLICY

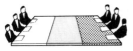

EUROPEAN PARLIAMENT
KEEPS A CLOSE WATCH
ON THE COMMISSIONS

COURT OF JUSTICE
SETTLES DISPUTES

*To be merged into one

refused to join E.C.S.C. and a year later, E.D.C. Whilst willing to play a part in European defence through N.A.T.O.,
Britain was still not convinced by the late 1950s of the need to
'join' Europe or even of the wisdom of doing so. The Six were
very keen to have Britain join E.E.C. and Euratom, particularly since she led the world in the peaceful development of
atomic energy. One leading 'European' is reported to have
said that Britain could have joined on her 'own terms' before
1958.

Britain sent two observers to Messina and sat in on the
Spaak Committee, playing an active part in discussions. Then

opposition to supranationalism reappeared and Britain withdrew from the Committee. Instead, late in 1956, she proposed a free trade area covering all O.E.E.C. states. This would have meant a customs union *without* the common market external tariff decided in the Treaty of Rome. Although it was shown possible to link the E.E.C. to a larger free trade area, the French refused to agree to it. This was because their foodstuffs cost more than products of the British Commonwealth and if those products were allowed to enter freely it would have hurt French farmers seriously. At the end of 1958 the British proposal was firmly rejected. E.E.C. was by this time established. Once again Britain had 'missed the boat' to Europe.

The European Free Trade Association (E.F.T.A.)

Although the European Community is primarily concerned with the economic development of its members, many hope that it will one day lead to a political union; that is one government instead of six. The failure of Britain's plan for a free trade area brought her close to the five other European powers opposed to supranationalism—Sweden, Norway, Denmark, Switzerland and Austria. These five and Britain all favoured a free trade area and, encouraged by major industrialists, their governments began active negotiations in the winter of 1958–9. Portugal joined the talks, which led to the name of the 'outer seven' being given to the group.

E.F.T.A. meeting in London

If Britain seriously hoped to join E.E.C. at this stage it is difficult to understand why she tied herself up with neutral, low-tariff countries of the 'outer seven'. The combined population of Britain's partners in the seven was only 38 million compared to the 170 million of E.E.C. Therefore, Britain was gaining little compared to say Sweden which was getting over Britain's high tariff wall to a market of 54 million.

Nevertheless, ministers from the 'outer seven' met at Stockholm in July 1959 to found the European Free Trade Association (E.F.T.A.). Finland became an associate in 1961.

It was agreed at Stockholm that tariffs would be abolished by approximately 10 per cent per annum from 1960 to 1970. This timetable was later speeded up so that all tariffs were eventually abolished by 1 January 1967, except in Portugal where they will remain until 1980. This applied only to industrial goods and not to agricultural products. A lot of debating time was taken up deciding whether frozen fish fillets were industrial goods. The Norwegians supported by the other fishing nations managed to persuade Britain that they were. Agreements between individual countries have since been signed to provide for trade in agricultural products; for example, Danish dairy products find their biggest market in Britain.

Trade amongst E.F.T.A. countries increased by 95 per cent between 1959 and 1965 compared with 38 per cent in the previous six years. This was generally satisfactory but less so for Britain. Although Britain's trade with E.F.T.A. countries increased by 72 per cent between 1958 and 1964, her trade with E.E.C. rose by 98 per cent. It was probably obvious to the British Government within a year or so of the establishment of E.F.T.A. that the thirty-eight million market offered was no substitute for the possibilities in E.E.C., over four times larger.

The New European Communities

EURATOM

The main purpose of Euratom is to produce cheap electricity from atomic energy. It has been estimated that the Six will need four times as much power by 1980 as they did in 1960.

To avoid the immense cost of increased fuel imports, particularly oil, it is hoped that cheap nuclear power can be made available. Nuclear power could save the community £8,000 million by A.D. 2000. The five-man Euratom commission has a Scientific and Technical Committee to advise it consisting of twenty of Europe's leading atom scientists and electrical engineers. Most of Euratom's research is carried out at Ispra in the Italian Alps by 1,400 scientists and technicians. There

Euratom Research Centre at Ispra

are other establishments in Holland, Belgium and Germany employing a further 600. By the mid-sixties several big projects were being developed, working on a budget of £230 million.

Whilst mainly concerned with nuclear power projects Euratom is also developing nuclear propulsion for ships and radio-isotopes. The latter have a variety of industrial and agricultural uses such as locating blockages in pipelines.

Euratom is also the sole purchaser and supplier of fissile material to the Six. Links have been established between Euratom and the atomic energy authorities of the U.S.A., Britain and Canada.

All work with nuclear materials involves danger. In 1959 basic health standards were approved for all workers in Euratom centres and inspectors were appointed to check on radiation levels throughout the countries of the Six. Since an accident could lead to enormous damage, each government gives insurance up to £24 million and could obtain a further £18 million from other European countries if required.

It is much too early to make judgments on the success of Euratom. It is worth noting, however, that one political writer[1] has called it 'an acknowledged fiasco', blaming the selfishness of member nations, particularly the French.

THE COMMON MARKET

Although General de Gaulle held up the development of supranationalism in the European Community, it is generally agreed that the Common Market has made a successful start. The following table shows various aspects of the economic development of E.E.C. between 1958 and 1964 compared with Britain.

	E.E.C. (%)	Britain (%)
Gross National Product	+68	+36
Industrial production	+49	+31
Inter-community trade	+168	+97
Exports to rest of world	+29	+28
Share of total world exports	+4	+1
Gold and foreign currency reserves	+64	−26
Income per head of population	+51	+23
Unemployment	−51	

These figures do not prove that E.E.C. has succeeded since Austria, not a member of the Community, has enjoyed an even faster rate of growth. But as Professor Hallstein, President of the E.E.C. Commission, has remarked, 'they certainly show that E.E.C. has not failed'.

Perhaps another indication of the potential of E.E.C. can be seen from the attitude of American businessmen. In 1956

[1] Nora Beloff, *The Observer*, 7 January 1967.

£86 million of American capital was invested in the Six. In
1963 the corresponding figure was over £250 million. It is also
worth noting that by 1963 over 600 American companies had
established themselves in E.E.C.

While money has crossed frontiers with ease, workers of the
Six seem reluctant to move out of their homelands. By 1962
less than 600,000 had moved to another country of the Community out of a total work force of seventy-five million. A large
percentage of these were in West Germany which also employs
about 200,000 non-Germans from outside the Community.
Trade union federations were quick to realise the need for
change, and have set up supranational organisations in
Brussels and Luxembourg.

The need for workers to move away from home may be
decreased by the establishment of new industries in underdeveloped parts of E.E.C. This is the responsibility of the
European Investment Bank which has a capital of £40
million. Southern Italy has benefited most. In Taranto steel,
cement and metal works and an oil refinery have brought new
life to an unemployment black spot.

AGRICULTURE IN E.E.C.

The Treaty of Rome stated that there should be a 'common
agricultural policy' in E.E.C. but did not state in detail how
this should be achieved. It is easy to see why the Treaty was so
vague. Agriculture has been a major source of worry to
European governments since the depression of 1875–96. The
two world wars showed the need to be able to produce a large
part of one's own food requirements. Yet most of Western
Europe's farms are small family businesses of less than 25 acres,
and therefore not easy to modernise. This can be shown by the
fact that in the period 1950–60 agricultural production increased by only 25 per cent compared to industry's 40 per cent.
For nearly 100 years governments sought to protect their own
agriculture by charging heavy duties on imported food. Then
at a time when food prices throughout the world were falling
the Spaak Committee was proposing to end protection.

The Treaty of Rome called for a fair standard of living for
the agricultural population, reasonable prices for the con-

sumer and a steady guaranteed market. After many months of negotiations and planning a European agricultural code was adopted by the Council of Ministers on 14 January 1962. This stated that a Common Market for agricultural produce would be gradually set up between 1 August 1962 and 31 December 1969. This meant that after 1970 Community foodstuffs could circulate freely at a common price.

To protect farmers a duty is charged on imported foods which is paid by each country into a central fund while a subsidy is given to help food exports. The European Agricultural Guidance and Guarantee Fund has been set up to deal with the price mechanism, to purchase surplus foodstuffs and to help with the modernisation of agriculture.

Britain Rejected

BRITAIN AND E.E.C.—2

Exactly one year to the day after the success of signing the European agricultural code, E.E.C. suffered its first great crisis. Speaking at a press conference, General de Gaulle announced that Britain was not ready to accept the conditions of membership of E.E.C. as he understood them. In spite of the intercession of Dr Adenauer and others, de Gaulle would not change his mind. On 29 January 1963 Britain's first attempt to enter E.E.C. came to an end.

Harold Macmillan had announced Britain's decision to seek entry into E.E.C. some eighteen months previously in an address to the House of Commons. Edward Heath, later the Conservative Party Leader, was put in charge of negotiations with the Six which began in Brussels on 10 October 1961. 'We desire to become full, whole-hearted and active members of the European Community in its widest sense', said Mr Heath, but there were many difficulties to be solved first.

The first and perhaps greatest problem was the future of the Commonwealth if Britain joined E.E.C. Before making his statement to the Commons in July 1961 Mr Macmillan sent his leading Ministers around the Commonwealth to discuss the decision to join E.E.C. Malaya, Pakistan and New Zealand thought it would be in Britain's interest to join,

The new E.E.C. Headquarters in Brussels

though the latter was very worried about its food exports to Britain. Australia, Canada, India and the African countries were opposed to Britain's entry in varying degrees and for various reasons.

However, in economic terms the Commonwealth has been of declining importance to Britain and vice versa. Between 1958 and 1964 British trade with the Commonwealth rose by only 1·6 per cent, while trade with E.E.C. rose by 98 per cent. This trend was obviously realised in 1962 when negotiations with E.E.C. were well under way. The real difficulty lay in the field of temperate zone foodstuffs imported from Australia, New Zealand and Canada. These came into Britain at preferential rates. Tied up with this was the problem of the £300 million per year paid by the British Government to its own farmers in the form of subsidies. The E.E.C. agricultural treaty does not permit agricultural subsidies. Nor could Britain expect to receive cheap food from the Commonwealth while the rest of E.E.C. built up a tariff wall against its products.

The other problem was the future of E.F.T.A. While Denmark and Norway could join E.E.C. easily, Finland and Austria were bound to political neutrality by international treaty. Portugal's weak economy would need protection. The real problem was the position of Sweden and Switzerland, both longstanding neutrals who disliked the idea of political union in Europe.

The main negotiations at Brussels adjourned for the summer of 1962 without having come to a firm agreement on British entry. Before they resumed a Commonwealth Prime Ministers' meeting was held in London. Almost without exception they expressed grave doubts for their own economic future and the political future of the Commonwealth.

In spite of these views, when negotiations were resumed at Brussels in October 1962 Mr Heath assured the Six that his policies were unchanged. He hoped to have everything settled before Christmas but the meeting adjourned on 20 December. During the break General de Gaulle called his famous news conference, closing the door on British entry.

WHY THE GENERAL SAID 'NO'

While the Brussels negotiations had been about economic problems, the General was mainly concerned with Britain's political role. He evidently believed that Britain was not truly 'European' but rather a leading member of the 'Anglo-Saxon' group (U.S.A., Canada, Australia, Scandinavia). He was not convinced that Britain had given up her pretensions to being a worldwide power, regarding Europe as a bunch of naughty children to be kept in check.

There was some truth in the General's point of view. During 1958 Britain had tried to undermine the Community idea by her free trade area proposals. Many influential Britons consistently opposed entry—including former Prime Ministers Attlee and Eden, Labour Party Leaders Hugh Gaitskell and Emanuel Shinwell and Lord Beaverbrook, who conducted a

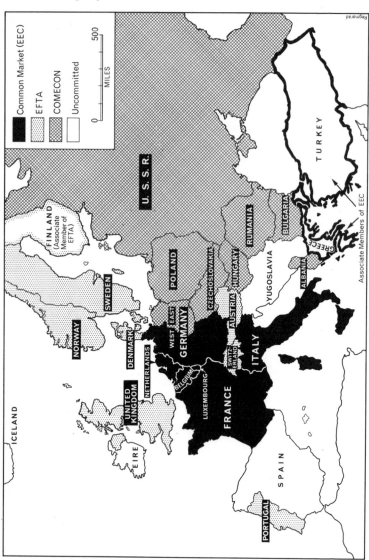

Economic Divisions of Europe: 1963

The United Kingdom, Ireland, Sweden and Denmark were added in 1973.

hysterical campaign through the *Express* newspapers. The final insult came during the negotiations in December 1962. At a meeting in the Bahamas, President Kennedy offered Polaris missiles to Macmillan as a replacement for the ageing V-bomber force. France had become a nuclear power in 1960, so if Britain had wished to prove that she was genuinely 'European', de Gaulle must have reasoned, why did she not offer to co-operate with France in the development of nuclear weapons? Instead Britain would be dependent on American goodwill for its nuclear striking power once the V-bombers were scrapped.

Critics of the General have said that the real reason for his refusal was his fear that France would be overshadowed in the Community. In particular he saw Europe as an independent power in the world equal in wealth and strength to the U.S.A. and Soviet Union. Presumably he thought Britain would be America's wooden horse inside the 'walls of Europe'.

European Co-operation

By 1975 it should be possible to fly across the Atlantic in three hours in the Concorde supersonic airliner. This plane is being built jointly by British and French aircraft firms. In October 1967 plans were announced for a joint British–French–German 275-seater 'air-bus'. These projects illustrate that co-operation has spread far beyond the bounds of E.E.C. and E.F.T.A. These have been mainly in social and advanced technological fields.

The first of these was the European Organisation for Nuclear Research (C.E.R.N.), founded in 1954 by twelve states. C.E.R.N. has its own laboratory in Geneva. Europe has also made its own modest contribution in space research. Ten states joined in 1964 to form the European Space Research Organisation (E.S.R.O.). Closely connected to E.S.R.O. is the European Launcher Development Organisation (E.L.D.O.), to which Britain has contributed the Blue Streak rocket as the first stage of Europa 1. By 1973 E.S.R.O. had virtually ceased operations and a new organisation, closely linked to the US space agency, was being planned by 10 nations.

The largest European-based organisation, founded in 1950,

is the European Broadcasting Union, with twenty-five members. In addition there are forty associate members outside Europe, including Japanese, Brazilian, American and Congolese companies. In 1954 Eurovision was established, enabling great events to be seen across the continent. These have included the 1964 Tokyo Olympics, the 1966 World Cup, the election of Pope Paul and several royal weddings. Eurovision has organised programmes of its own of which the best known is the Annual Song Contest.

There has been no lack of co-operation amongst European nations in the field of sport. Clubs from all over Europe compete in football competitions such as the Cup-Winners' Cup. The European Athletic Championships, held every three years, produce extremely high performances. Boxing, swimming and winter sports championships are keenly contested, but the English sports of rugby and cricket have found little favour across the Channel.

Since the mid-nineteenth century when railways came to Europe, co-operation in transport has been common practice. Lately the Six have established a network of high-speed luxury trains, the Trans-Europe Expresses, linking the major cities. Motorway building has lagged except perhaps in West Germany and has been devoted to national interests. The E.E.C. Commission has urged the Six to plan their motorways in conjunction. By 1980 it may be possible to drive by motorway from Scotland to Sicily via the Channel Tunnel.

BRITAIN AND E.E.C.—3

Early in 1967 Harold Wilson began a series of visits to the capitals of the Six with a view to seeking British entry into E.E.C.

On 11 May Britain's formal application for membership of E.E.C., E.C.S.C. and Euratom was presented at Brussels. The previous day Parliament had supported the application by 488 votes to 62. Denmark and Ireland applied simultaneously with Britain; Norway and Sweden followed suit two months later.

Five of the Six, West Germany, Italy, Belgium, the Netherlands and Luxembourg strongly supported the application of Britain and the other four countries. Again it was the attitude of France which caused doubt. Many thought that General de

Gaulle's attitude to Britain had changed in the four years since his veto on British membership. Speaking at a press conference five days after Britain's application, 16th May 1967, de Gaulle said 'The movement which seems to be leading England to link herself to Europe . . . can only be satisfactory to France. For our part there is no question of there being a veto nor has there ever been one'. He then went on to point out some of the obstacles to British entry; agriculture, Britain's economic problems, especially the role of sterling and her relationship with the U.S.A. and the Commonwealth.

Before the end of the year the riddle of the General's true position appeared to be solved. In November he called another press-conference at which he stated clearly that Britain was not yet ready for entry into E.E.C. Shortly afterwards the devaluation of the pound by 14·3 per cent seemed to justify the General's reluctance to admit the shaky British economy into the Community. During 1968 and 1969 the position of Britain and France began to change. Of all the Western nations France was most sorely shaken by the massive wave of revolutionary unrest which arose in 1968. In May Paris erupted with tremendous violence as thousands of students and striking workers joined forces against the government. The effect upon the French economy was disastrous and her gold reserves began rapidly draining away. Within a year de Gaulle had resigned and the French franc was devalued 11 per cent shortly afterwards.

By the middle of 1969 devaluation of the pound was beginning to give Britain a considerable improvement in exports and a strengthening of her economy.

THE ENLARGEMENT OF THE E.E.C., 1973

In May 1969 De Gaulle was succeeded as President by Georges Pompidou. At the Hague 'summit' meeting in December the leaders of the 'Six' agreed that, with Britain, Denmark, Ireland and Norway all seeking entry, it would be of benefit to have an enlarged Community.

After a meeting of Ministers at Luxemburg in June 1970 serious negotiations between the 'Six' and the 'Four' began the following October. For Britain there were a limited number of issues all relating to the Community's agricultural policy: Britain's share of the cost and the stages of payment over the years; how to protect New Zealand's dairy farmers and Commonwealth sugar producers who would lose their trading privileges and how many years Britain should take to become fully integrated into the system. Since France was the Community's largest agricultural producer her attitude was extremely important in the difficult negotiations.

In May 1971 Mr. Heath, the British Conservative Prime Minister since the previous June, and M. Pompidou, met in Paris and came to an agreement about the future of the EEC and other matters. With exceptions of fisheries regulations, a matter of the greatest importance to Norway, agreements were reached on special terms for N. Zealand and Commonwealth sugar during the first few years of British membership of the EEC.

On matters of voting and representation Britain was awarded equal rights with the three other major powers France, Germany and Italy. For the period 1973–7 Britain will pay approximately 20 per cent of the Community budget but will be entitled to various payments and subsidies in return.

On 28 October 1971 the British Parliament voted 356 to 244 in favour of joining. Those against entry were the majority (all but 69) of the Labour Party and 41 Conservatives. Each of the other three applicants held a referendum. In Ireland 84 per cent of the electors voted in favour of joining and in Denmark 63 per cent but in Norway 53.5 per cent rejected membership. Thus on 1 January 1973 the 'Six' became 'the Nine'.

7 Western Europe — into the Seventies

'*Two Empires will divide the world between them: Russia in the East and America in the West; and we, the people in between, shall be too degraded, sunk too low to know . . . what we have been*'— Baron Grimm, 1789

The Strength of Western Europe

Never in all her history has Western Europe been so rich, so productive and so powerful. West Germany, France and Britain are, apart from the two super-powers and Japan, the world's leading industrial and exporting nations. Italy's Ferraris long dominated motor-racing, while her civil engineers have produced many fine works, including the Kariba Dam. France's electric railways are probably the world's best, and her aircraft industry has successfully challenged the American giants. Swedish shipbuilders have a record second only to the amazing Japanese. Britain still leads the world in nuclear energy production, radar and electronic guidance, and is the only place outside the U.S.A. with a sizeable computer industry. West Germany's success in the motor and machine-tool industries is legendary. Even tiny Switzerland is world-famous for its watches and hydro-electric power stations. Denmark and Holland possess the finest agricultural and horticultural experts.

The West German army today possesses far greater striking power than did Hitler's legions in 1939. One British or French jet bomber or a nuclear submarine can inflict more damage than all the battleships of 1914 or the Wellingtons, Dorniers and Flying Fortresses of 1942.

The Decline of Europe

Yet at no time since her expansion began about A.D. 1500 has Europe been so relatively weak and unimportant in the world. In numbers alone, Europeans are outnumbered four to one by the rest of the world.

Although Europe's decline has become painfully clear only since 1945, the seeds of decay were sown seventy years ago. By 1900 the U.S.A. had overtaken both Britain and Germany in industrial production and was becoming a world power after defeating Spain. At the same time the Trans-Siberian Railway was bringing Russians to the Pacific. Russia herself was temporarily stopped by another rising power, Japan, which was to play a major role in destroying Europe's empires. The other Asian giant, China, was already moving towards independence and strength, even though under Western domination. Meanwhile Europeans were rushing blindly towards their suicidal civil war: 1917 marked the end of West European world supremacy when, in their exhaustion, the Allies called upon the young American giant for help. In the same year, the Russian revolution heralded the birth of the second super-power.

Yet the myth of European supremacy lasted until 1941 as both the Americans and Russians withdrew from the world stage leaving it free for the Fascist dictators and their Japanese allies. When war came again, the price of victory was paid for mainly in American money and Russian blood. Although Britain gallantly fought alone in 1940 she could no more have advanced to total victory alone than she could have done in 1917.

So 1945 came with Europe battered and crushed and the American and Soviet war machines standing face to face over the corpse of Nazi Germany. They face each other still, and although Europe has recovered completely and advanced far beyond her 1939 position, the shadows of the super-powers still cover the Continent. Meanwhile Europe's great source of glory and supposed power, her overseas empires, has disappeared. The European powers which once ruled these empires are now too small ever to play an individual world role.

It is to these former colonies that the centre of world

politics has moved. China, India, South-East Asia, particularly Vietnam, and the Middle East are now the world's most important places. If a major war does break out it is likely to start in Asia and not, as in 1914 and 1939, in Eastern Europe. Slightly less important is Southern Africa.

The Unity and Disunity of Europe

A visitor from a distant part of the world would see few major differences at first amongst the people of Western Europe. Fashions, apart from traditional costume, owe much to Italy, Paris and, of late, London. Volkswagens, Minis and Fiats struggle through jams in every major town. In many cases the historic towns are losing their national identities as tower blocks and prefabricated buildings rise above new motorways. Most Western Europeans are members of the Roman Catholic or of the Protestant Churches. They vote Socialist or Christian Democrat (Conservative), though both Liberals and Communists have strong followings in various countries. Most Western European countries operate welfare services to protect their citizens from the worst effects of sickness, unemployment and old age. Sport, television, the cinema and Mediterranean holidays have no national frontiers. Even the teenage problem is international. If Britain had its 'Mods and

Europeans supreme! The 1966 World Cup Final

Rockers', Germany has its 'Halbstark', Holland its 'Provos', Russia the 'Stilyagi'. In 1968 student riots swept Europe.

Yet our visitor would eventually begin to find differences other than the obvious one of language. The Iron Curtain still stands but every year traffic between East and West becomes freer. In spite of the millions of sun-seekers who cross the Pyrenees each year, Spain remains the outcast of Europe. Many cannot forget that Franco was the friend of Hitler and Mussolini. Some Britons, unable to forget the days of the Empire, would like to see their country a voluntary outcast from Europe. Sweden and Switzerland also cling to a form of isolationism.

The problem of a divided Germany has become considerably easier since the late 1960s. This has been very largely due to the efforts of one man—Willy Brandt. In 1966 Brandt, a popular and courageous anti-Nazi became vice-Chancellor and Foreign Minister of West Germany in 1969 Chancellor. He immediately began seeking better relations with East Germany, Poland and the U.S.S.R. Meetings of the respective leaders were held throughout 1969–73 in Bonn, Erfurt, Kassel, Moscow and Warsaw. There Brandt knelt before the memorial of the Warsaw Ghetto, the last refuge of the Jews which the SS had destroyed in 1943.

Talks between East and West Germany were the least successful. In August 1970 a treaty was signed between the U.S.S.R. and West Germany promising to settle all disputes peacefully and agreeing that the present frontiers of Europe should remain unchanged. In Warsaw in December 1970 a similar document was signed by Poland and West Germany. These became 'official' in 1972. Meanwhile the 'Big Four' had drawn up a new treaty on Berlin allowing free access and this was also signed by the two Germanys.

For his work in improving East-West relations Willy Brandt was awarded the Nobel Peace Prize in 1971. In the Federal Election of November 1972 his S.P.D. party increased its vote by 3 per cent (6 seats) as did its partners the F.D.P. (11 seats). In June 1973 the Security Council recommended that both East and West Germany be admitted to the U.N.O. By the early 1970s West Germany was establishing itself as a strong influence for peace in Europe.

Biographical Notes

ADENAUER, Konrad (1876–1967)
German politician. Mayor of Cologne 1917–33 and 1945. Arrested by Nazis 1934 and 1944. Chairman of C.D.U. in British Zone 1946. Chancellor of West Germany 1949–63. Anti-Communist and strong supporter of Western European unity.

ATTLEE, Clement (1883–1967)
British politician. Barrister and lecturer 1906–23. Labour M.P. 1922–55. Leader of Labour Party 1935–55. Deputy Prime Minister 1942–5. Prime Minister 1945–51. Created Earl in 1955.

BEVIN, Ernest (1881–1951)
British politician. Began work at thirteen. Full-time trade unionist 1911. Formed massive Transport and General Workers Union 1922. Labour M.P. 1940. Minister of Labour 1940–5. Foreign Secretary 1945–51. Strong supporter of U.N.O. and Western Alliances.

CHURCHILL, Winston (1874–1965)
British politician. Army officer 1895–1900 and 1916–17. Conservative M.P. 1900–5, Liberal 1906–22, Conservative 1924–64. Held many government posts 1905–29. Recalled to Admiralty 1939. Prime Minister 1940–5 and 1951–5.

DE GASPERI, Alcide (1881–1954)
Italian politician. Journalist. Deputy to Austrian Parliament 1919 and Italian 1921–4. Imprisoned by Mussolini 1926–7. Prime Minister 1945–52 and leader of Christian Democrats. Foreign Minister 1951–3. Strong supporter of European unity.

DE GAULLE, Charles (1890–1970)
French politician and soldier. Captain during World War I. Strong supporter of armoured warfare. Chief of Free French 1940–4. President of provisional Government 1944–6. Prime Minister 1958–9. President of France 1959–69.

EDEN, Robert Anthony (1897–)
British politician. Infantry officer during World War I. Conservative M.P. 1923–57. Foreign Secretary 1935–8, 1940–5, 1951–5. Prime Minister 1955–7. Now Earl of Avon.

EISENHOWER, Dwight David (1890–1969)
American soldier and politician. U.S. Commander-in-Chief Europe 1942–5. Military Governor U.S. Zone of Germany 1945. Supreme Allied Commander 1949–52. President of United States 1953–61.

ERHARD, Ludwig (1897–)
German economist and politician. Minister of Trade and Industry, Bavaria 1945. Organised currency reform 1948. Economics Minister 1949–63. Chancellor of West Germany 1963–6.

KENNEDY, John Fitzgerald (1917–63)
American politician. U.S. Navy 1941–5, wounded and decorated. U.S. House of Representatives 1946–52 and Senate 1952–61. President of United States 1961–3. Assassinated.

KHRUSHCHEV, Nikita Sergeyevich (1894–1971)
Soviet politician. Engine fitter in Donbass coalfield. Joined Communists 1918. Secretary of Moscow Party 1935–8. Served on Ukraine front 1941–5. First Secretary of Soviet Communist Party 1953–64. Prime Minister 1959–64.

MACMILLAN, Harold (1894–)
British politician. Guards Captain 1914–18. Conservative M.P. 1924–9 and 1931–64. Foreign Secretary 1955. Prime Minister 1957–63.

POMPIDOU, Georges Jean Raymond (1911–)
French politician, Gaullist Party, formerly teacher and merchant banker (Rothschild) Prime Minister 1962–8. President of the Republic 1969–

SPAAK, Paul-Henri (1899–)
Belgian politician. Socialist deputy. Prime Minister of Belgium 1938–9, 1947–9. Secretary-General of N.A.T.O. 1957–61. Promoter of Benelux and Treaties of Brussels and Rome.

TITO, Josip Broz (1892–)
Yugoslav politician. Austrian army 1913–15. Trade union leader 1920–8. Secretary-General Yugoslav Communist Party 1937. Resistance leader 1941–5. President of Yugoslavia 1945–

Abbreviations

Benelux	Belgium, Netherlands and Luxemburg.
C.D.U.*	Christian Democratic Union.
C.E.R.N.*	European Organisation for Nuclear Research.
C.F.M.	Council of Foreign Ministers.
Comecon	Council for Mutual Economic Assistance.
Cominform	Communist Information Bureau.
D.D.R.*	(East) German Democratic Republic.
E.A.C.	European Advisory Commission.
E.A.M.*	National Liberation Front.
E.B.U.	European Broadcasting Union.
E.C.S.C.	European Coal and Steel Community.
E.D.C.	European Defence Community.
E.D.E.S.*	Greek Democratic National League.
E.E.C.	European Economic Community (Common Market).
E.F.T.A.	European Free Trade Association.
E.L.A.S.*	National People's Liberation Army.
E.L.D.O.	European Launcher Development Organisation.
E.P.U.	European Payments Union.
E.R.P.	European Recovery Programme.
E.S.R.O.	European Space Research Organisation.
Euratom	European Atomic Energy Community.
F.D.P.*	Free Democrats (West Germany).
F.D.R.	Federal Republic of (West) Germany.
F.L.N.*	National Liberation Front.
G.A.T.T.	General Agreement on Tariffs and Trade.
K.P.D.*	German Communist Party.
N.A.T.O.	North Atlantic Treaty Organisation.
O.A.S.*	Secret Army Organisation.
O.E.C.D.	Organisation for Economic Co-operation and Development.
O.E.E.C.	Organisation for European Economic Co-operation.
S.P.D.*	Social Democrat Party (West Germany).

155

U.N.O.   United Nations Organisation.
U.N.R.R.A.   United Nations Relief and Rehabilitation
             Administration.
V.S.O.   Voluntary Service Overseas.
W.E.U.   Western European Union.

* Initials of language concerned.

European Membership of International Organisations
(including associates)

	U.N.O.	Council of Europe	O.E.C.D.	E.E.C.	E.F.T.A.	COMECON	N.A.T.O.	W.E.U.	Warsaw Pact	Eurovision
Albania	*					*			*	
Austria	*	*	*		*					*
Belgium	*	*	*	*			*	*		*
Bulgaria	*					*			*	*
Czechoslovakia	*					*			*	*
Denmark	*	*	*	*			*			*
Finland	*		*		*					*
France	*	*	*	*			*	*		*
Germany, East	*					*			*	*
Germany, West	*	*	*	*			*	*		*
Greece	*	*	*	*			*			*
Hungary	*					*			*	*
Iceland	*	*	*				*			*
Ireland	*	*	*	*						*
Italy	*	*	*	*			*	*		*
Luxembourg	*	*	*	*			*	*		*
Malta	*	*								
Netherlands	*	*	*	*			*	*		*
Norway	*	*	*		*		*			*
Poland	*					*			*	*
Portugal	*		*		*		*			*
Rumania	*					*			*	*
Spain	*		*							*
Sweden	*	*	*		*					*
Switzerland		*	*		*					
Turkey	*	*	*	*			*			
U.S.S.R.	*					*			*	*
United Kingdom	*	*	*	*			*	*		*
Yugoslavia	*		*			*				*

Abbreviations

State	Area (sq. kms)	Population (millions)	Capital city	Economy	Politics	Major Religion
Albania	28,748	2·1	Tiranë	A	C	M
Austria	83,849	7·3	Vienna	A	WN	R
Belgium	30,497	9·7	Brussels	I	W	R
Bulgaria	110,861	8·5	Sofia	A	C	O
Czechoslovakia	127,866	14·4	Prague	I	C	R
Denmark	44,446	4·9	Copenhagen	A	W	P
Finland	337,000	4·7	Helsinki	A	WN	P
France	550,986	50·8	Paris	I	W	R
Germany, East	108,173	15·9	Berlin	I	C	P
Germany, West	248,574	59·3	Bonn	I	W	R
Greece	132,737	8·7	Athens	A	W	O
Hungary	93,011	10·3	Budapest	A	C	R
Iceland	102,846	0·2	Reykjavik	F	W	P
Ireland	82,460	2·9	Dublin	A	WN	R
Italy	301,225	54·6	Rome	I	W	R
Luxembourg	2,586	0·3	Luxembourg	I	W	R
Malta	317	0·3	Valletta	A	W	R
Netherlands	33,778	13·0	Amsterdam	A	W	P
Norway	323,878	3·9	Oslo	F	W	P
Poland	312,520	32·9	Warsaw	A	C	R
Portugal	88,860	9·6	Lisbon	A	W	R
Rumania	237,500	20·0	Bucharest	A	C	O
Spain	490,774	33·3	Madrid	A	WN	R
Sweden	449,793	8·0	Stockholm	I	WN	P
Switzerland	41,288	6·3	Berne	I	WN	P
Turkey*	771,820	32·5	Ankara	A	W	M
U.S.S.R.*	22,402,200	241·7	Moscow	I	C	O
United Kingdom	243,973	55·5	London	I	W	P
Yugoslavia	256,580	21·5	Belgrade	A	CN	O

A = Agricultural
C = Communist
CN = Communist Neutral
F = Fishing
I = Industrial
M = Muslim

O = Orthodox
P = Protestant
R = Roman Catholic
W = Western Alliance
WN = Western Neutral
* Including territories in Asia.

Further Reading

There is an enormous selection of books dealing with the events of the last quarter-century. The majority are for adults but fifth-formers will benefit from studying some of the following books:

Background Reading

R. C. MOWAT, *Ruin and Resurgence 1939–65*. Blandford Press, 1966.

L. JAMES, *Europe*. Blackwell, 1965.

J. GUNTHER, *Inside Europe Today*. Hamish Hamilton, 1962.

D. W. UNWIN, *Western Europe Since 1945*. Longman 1968.

S. DE LA MAHOTIÉRE, *Towards one Europe*. Penguin, 1970.

A. SAMPSON, *The New Europeans*. Hodder & Stoughton 1968, Panther, 1971.

W. LAQUEUR, *Europe Since Hitler*. Weidenfeld and Nicholson, 1970. Pelican, 1972.

W. KNAPP, *A History of War and Peace*. Oxford University Press, 1967.

Special Topics

J. ARDAGH, *The New France*. Penguin 1973.

A. WERTH, *De Gaulle*. Penguin, 1966.

E. CRANKSHAW, *Khrushchev*. Collins, 1966.

R. RODRIGO, *Berlin Blockade*. Cassell, 1960.

M. BALFOUR, *West Germany*. Benn 1968.

H. THOMAS, *Suez Affair*. Weidenfeld, Nicholson 1967. Penguin 1970.

L. B. BAIN, *Reluctant Satellites*. Macmillan of New York, 1960.

J. ROY, *The Battle of Dienbienphu*. Faber, 1965.

J. HATCH, *A History of Post-War Africa*. Methuen, 1967.

D. DONNELLY, *The Struggle for the World*. Collins, 1965.

R. C. MOWAT, *Creating the European Community*. Blandford 1973.

Index

Index